Credits

Author

Rhawi Dantas

Reviewers

Adam Dudczak

Laurenţiu Matei

Holger Stenzhorn

Acquisition Editor

Chaitanya Apte

Development Editor

Roger D'Souza

Technical Editor

Pallavi Kachare

Copy Editor

Kriti Sharma

Project Coordinator

Jovita Pinto

Proofreader

Dan McMahon

Indexer

Hemangini Bari

Production Coordinator

Aparna Bhagat

Cover Work

Aparna Bhagat

About the Author

Rhawi Dantas is a Brazilian Software Engineer, more specifically from Recife, with severeal years of experience in the Java platform. He has mainly focused on Web/Server developmen and hsa contributed to projects ranging from mobile/server integration, different customization of IDEs and development of CRMs. He currently works at `Paf.com` with Java Web development.

He graduated as Bachelor in Information Systems and at that time he had the opportunity to work as a tutor for the University with Object Oriented Programming subject. Besides full-time work he is on his way with his Masters in Software Systems at the Tampere University of Technology.

He is also certified as SCJP, SCWCD, and SCSNI.

This is a small thank you to the three most important women in my life: Sônia Dantas, Paula Mäkinen-Dantas, and Maria Dantas. I would also like to thank the work of my editors, especially Jovita Pinto and Roger D'Souza, and all of the reviewers for their valuable contribution.

NetBeans IDE 7 Cookbook

Over 70 highly focused practical recipes to maximize your output with NetBeans

Rhawi Dantas

BIRMINGHAM - MUMBAI

NetBeans IDE 7 Cookbook

First published: May 2011

Production Reference: 1200511

Published by Packt Publishing Ltd.
32 Lincoln Road
Olton
Birmingham, B27 6PA, UK.

ISBN 978-1-849512-50-3

www.packtpub.com

Cover Image by Ed Maclean (edmaclean@gmail.com)

About the Reviewers

Adam Dudczak works as a computer programmer and researcher in Poznan Supercomputing and Networking Center. He is an experienced Java developer who has a broad experience in building large-scale content management systems. He has co-authored several papers in the field of digital libraries, information retrieval, and text mining.

Adam is a leader of the Poznan Java User Group (http://www.jug.poznan.pl), and has organized numerous local Java-related events including Poznan NetBeans day and NetBeans Platform training. He is also a member of the GeeCON conference (http:/geecon.org) organizing committee.

In his free time he teaches Java development at Poznan University of Technology and writes a blog: http://dudczak.info/dry.

Laurenţiu Matei holds a master's degree in Systems and Computer Science from Politehnica University in Bucharest.

He works for MrSwing, a financial software company, as senior developer and for 8Seconds, an e-mail optimization company, as head of research and development.

His main interests are web development, clustering, and multi-tier architecture.

His best skills are combined in the open source project Chartsy.org, a stock trading, screening and charting platform based on the NetBeans Platform.

Holger Stenzhorn studied computational linguistics at Saarland University in Saarbrücken, Germany and is currently a research associate at the Department of Paediatric Oncology and Hematology of the Saarland University Hospital in Homburg, Germany. Before, he had positions as a researcher at the Institute for Medical Biometry and Medical Informatics of the Freiburg University Medical Center, Germany and the Institute of Formal Ontology and Medical Information Science in Saarbrücken, Germany, and he was also visiting researcher at the Digital Enterprise Research Institute in Galway, Ireland, before he worked as a software engineer at XtraMind Technologies in Saarbrücken, Germany.

His work focuses on the representation and management of information and data, ontologies and Semantic Web technologies, biomedical informatics, natural language processing, user interfaces and software design and development. In the past he has participated in the development of multilingual document retrieval, information extraction, and natural language generation systems, both in industry and academia.

He has been involved in several ontology engineering and application tasks: an ontology for clinical trials on nephroblastoma and breast cancer (EU-funded ACGT project), an ontology for the research on cerebral aneurysms (EU-funded @neurIST project) as well as the BioTop top-domain ontology. His main work at the moment focuses on developing a software system (ObTiMA) for the improved management of clinical trials. Further, he is a member of the Healthcare and Life Sciences Interest Group of the World Wide Web Consortium.

www.PacktPub.com

Support files, eBooks, discount offers and more

You might want to visit www.PacktPub.com for support files and downloads related to your book.

Did you know that Packt offers eBook versions of every book published, with PDF and ePub files available? You can upgrade to the eBook version at www.PacktPub.com and as a print book customer, you are entitled to a discount on the eBook copy. Get in touch with us at service@packtpub.com for more details.

At www.PacktPub.com, you can also read a collection of free technical articles, sign up for a range of free newsletters and receive exclusive discounts and offers on Packt books and eBooks.

http://PacktLib.PacktPub.com

Do you need instant solutions to your IT questions? PacktLib is Packt's online digital book library. Here, you can access, read and search across Packt's entire library of books.

Why Subscribe?

- ▶ Fully searchable across every book published by Packt
- ▶ Copy and paste, print and bookmark content
- ▶ On demand and accessible via web browser

Free Access for Packt account holders

If you have an account with Packt at www.PacktPub.com, you can use this to access PacktLib today and view nine entirely free books. Simply use your login credentials for immediate access.

Table of Contents

Preface

Welcome to the NetBeans Cookbook.

NetBeans is a Java Integrated Development Environment, IDE, which enables fast application development with the most adopted frameworks, technologies, and servers.

Different than other IDEs, NetBeans comes already pre-packaged with a wide range of functionality out of the box, such as support for different frameworks, servers, databases, and mobile development.

This book does require a minimal knowledge of Java platform, more specifically the language ifself. But the book might as well be used by either beginners, who are trying to dip their toes in new technology, or more experienced developers, who are trying to switch from other IDEs but want to decrease their learning curve of a new environment. NetBeans integrates so many different technologies, many of which are present in this book, that it is beyond the scope of this book to cover all of them in depth. We provide the reader with links and information where to go when further knowledge is required.

What this book covers

Chapter 1, NetBeans Head First introduces the developer to the basics of NetBeans by creating basic Java projects and importing Eclipse or Maven projects.

Chapter 2, Basic IDE Usage covers the creation of packages, classes, and constructors, as well as some usability feature.

Chapter 3, Designing Desktop GUI Applications goes through the process of creating a desktop application, then connecting it to a database and even modifying it to look more professional.

Chapter 4, JDBC and NetBeans helps the developer to setup NetBeans with the most common database systems on the market and shows some of the functionality built-in to NetBeans for handling SQL.

Chapter 5, Building Web Applications introduces the usage of web frameworks such as JSF, Struts, and GWT.3

Chapter 6, Using JavaFX explains the basic of JavaFX application states and connecting our JavaFX app to a web service interface.

Chapter 7, EJB Application goes through the process of building an EJB application which supports JPA, stateless, and stateful beans and sharing a service through a web service interface.

Chapter 8, Mobile Development teaches how to create your own CLDC or CDC applications with the help of NetBeans Visual Mobile Designer.

Chapter 9, Java Refactoring lets NetBeans refactor your code to extract classes, interfaces, encapsulate fields, and other options.

Chapter 10, Extending the IDE includes handy examples on how to create your own panels and wizards so you can extend the functionality of the IDE.

Chapter 11, Profiling and Testing covers NetBeans Profiler, HTTP Monitor, and integration with tools that analyze code quality and load generator.

Chapter 12, Version Control shows how to configure NetBeans to be used with the most common version control systems on the market.

What you need for this book

Both Java Development Toolkit and NetBeans are essential for this book.

Follow the link below for the Java SDK:

`http://www.oracle.com/technetwork/java/javase/downloads/index.html`

And the one below for NetBeans:

`http://netbeans.org/downloads/index.html`

Note that since Oracle has decided not to include JavaFX development in the 7.0 release of NetBeans the 6.9.1 is required when doing the examples contained in the Using JavaFX chapter.

Here is the link for NetBeans 6.9.1:

`http://netbeans.org/community/releases/69/`

Other frameworks and tools, when required, are listed in the Introduction section of the recipe.

Who this book is for

This book is for everyone that wants to try NetBeans or is beginning with a new technology and would like an uncomplicated way to setup and start coding.

Familiarity with the Java programming language is required but examples contained in this book will range from basic concepts, like creating a class, to more advanced ones, like using different web frameworks or debugging an application.

Conventions

In this book, you will find a number of styles of text that distinguish between different kinds of information. Here are some examples of these styles, and an explanation of their meaning.

Code words in text are shown as follows: "The `MouseAdapter` is the interface which is used by the triggered event when a mouse is clicked."

A block of code is set as follows:

```
String firstName;
String lastName;
String maritialStatus;
int id;
int accountNumber;
```

When we wish to draw your attention to a particular part of a code block, the relevant lines or items are set in bold:

```
jButton1.addMouseListener(new java.awt.event.MouseAdapter() {
    public void mouseClicked(java.awt.event.MouseEvent evt) {
    jButton1MouseClicked(evt);
    }
});
```

New terms and **important words** are shown in bold. Words that you see on the screen, in menus or dialog boxes for example, appear in the text like this: "Leave all the other options marked and click **Finish**".

 Warnings or important notes appear in a box like this.

 Tips and tricks appear like this.

Reader feedback

Feedback from our readers is always welcome. Let us know what you think about this book—what you liked or may have disliked. Reader feedback is important for us to develop titles that you really get the most out of.

To send us general feedback, simply send an e-mail to feedback@packtpub.com, and mention the book title via the subject of your message.

If there is a book that you need and would like to see us publish, please send us a note in the **SUGGEST A TITLE** form on www.packtpub.com or e-mail suggest@packtpub.com.

If there is a topic that you have expertise in and you are interested in either writing or contributing to a book, see our author guide on www.packtpub.com/authors.

Customer support

Now that you are the proud owner of a Packt book, we have a number of things to help you to get the most from your purchase.

Downloading the example code

You can download the example code files for all Packt books you have purchased from your account at http://www.PacktPub.com. If you purchased this book elsewhere, you can visit http://www.PacktPub.com/support and register to have the files e-mailed directly to you.

Errata

Although we have taken every care to ensure the accuracy of our content, mistakes do happen. If you find a mistake in one of our books—maybe a mistake in the text or the code—we would be grateful if you would report this to us. By doing so, you can save other readers from frustration and help us improve subsequent versions of this book. If you find any errata, please report them by visiting http://www.packtpub.com/support, selecting your book, clicking on the **errata submission form** link, and entering the details of your errata. Once your errata are verified, your submission will be accepted and the errata will be uploaded on our website, or added to any list of existing errata, under the Errata section of that title. Any existing errata can be viewed by selecting your title from http://www.packtpub.com/support.

Piracy

Piracy of copyright material on the Internet is an ongoing problem across all media. At Packt, we take the protection of our copyright and licenses very seriously. If you come across any illegal copies of our works, in any form, on the Internet, please provide us with the location address or website name immediately so that we can pursue a remedy.

Please contact us at `copyright@packtpub.com` with a link to the suspected pirated material.

We appreciate your help in protecting our authors, and our ability to bring you valuable content.

Questions

You can contact us at `questions@packtpub.com` if you are having a problem with any aspect of the book, and we will do our best to address it.

1

NetBeans Head First

In this chapter, we will cover:

- ► Creating a Java Project using Wizard
- ► Creating libraries
- ► Sharing libraries
- ► Importing Projects from Eclipse
- ► Importing existing Maven Projects

Introduction

How to start a project successfully is often overlooked, but is always important. Projects often consist of many components that are built separately and then combined together to create a larger system. Because of this, we will look at how to create and share **libraries** so we can benefit from modularity and a more decentralized system. This will also help in configuring your environment to work with, for example, checking project folders into and out of version control systems.

Due to the decentralized nature of software engineering, we will take a look at how to import projects from different sources. This will give us a greater opportunity to work with various teams that use different sets of tools while still benefiting from NetBeans's capabilities.

Creating a Java Project Using Wizard

Let's start with a Java project. There is not much configuration to be done with this kind of project, but this will help in familiarizing with the IDE. It will also will give some insight on how to create other, more advanced projects since the flow is almost identical.

Getting ready

If you do not have NetBeans installed on your machine yet, please visit:

`http://netbeans.org`

It is also necessary to have Java installed; please visit: `http://www.oracle.com/technetwork/java/javase/downloads/index.html`

How to do it...

1. Let's create a New Project. This can be achieved by either clicking **File** and then **New Project**, or by pressing *Ctrl+Shift+N*.

2. In the **New Project** window, two panes will be shown. Choose **Java** on the **Categories** pane and **Java Application** on the **Proejcts** pane, then click **Next**.

3. At the **Name and Location** step, **Project Name** should be filled with `HelloWorld`.

4. At **Create Main Class**, append **com** to the beginning of `helloworld.Main`, giving `com.helloworld.Main`.

5. Leave all the other options marked and click **Finish**.

The configuration window should look like the following screenshot:

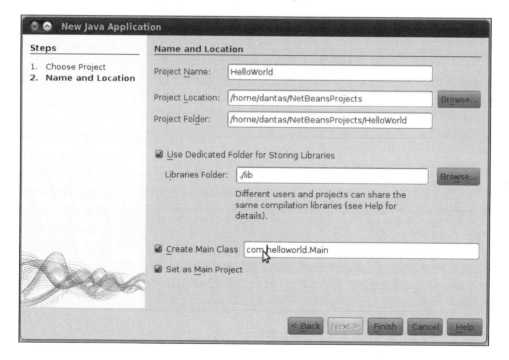

How it works...

While the project location can be specified, since we did not change the folder, NetBeans automatically adds the project to **NetBeansProjects**, which is the NetBeans default project folder.

Use dedicated Folder for Storing Libraries is marked since we would like to have a specific project folder where all of the libraries will be stored, making packaging and distribution easier in the future. Libraries are packaged as JAR files. A JAR file is an example of a library that contains Java sources, which enable the developer to extend the functionality of applications.

NetBeans will automatically generate a main class called Main, add a `main()` method, and generate default comments through the class when the **Create Main Class** option is marked.

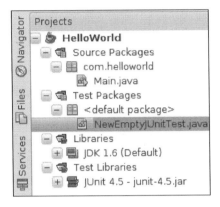

NetBeans will create the package structure, which will consist of Source Packages and Test Packages. The code templates provided by the IDE will correctly place the files in their respective folders. For example, if one JUnit test is created, the file will be placed under the **Test Packages** folder automatically.

One node containing libraries will also be shown in the projects view. This is where NetBeans will copy the necessary libraries. In the Java project, for example, NetBeans copies and configures the JUnit libraries into our newly-created project by default. Different projects will have different dependencies.

There's more...

You should play a bit with other project wizards. Most of the popular frameworks are supported in NetBeans IDE. It is good to get to know them.

Creating libraries

We will create a library folder upon project creation. For this recipe, we will create a Java EE project.

A library consists of a set of files that are packaged inside a compressed file. Many files can exist inside a library but usually, in Java, libraries contain only class, JARs, and configuration files. Libraries in Java can have different extensions.

Libraries in Java can have different extensions:

▶ **JAR**: An acronym for Java Archive. This file extension is built on top of a normal ZIP file to aggregate various files.

▶ **WAR**: Web Application Archive means that this file is responsible for obtaining Web Application related files. Example: images, Java files, JSPs, Servlets, XMLs, other JARs, and so on.

▶ **EAR**: The Enterprise Archive usually encompasses all the other files combined. Normally it contains other WARs (and will also hold the same file types), configuration types, and other JARs. This file is better suited to compact into a single file, many different modules of an application.

Both WAR and EAR are built on top of JAR. These files will be explored in future recipes so for now we will only work with normal JAR files.

Getting ready

Please refer to the *Getting ready* section of the previous recipe for necessary tools and configurations.

Once that is complete, it is possible to continue to the next section.

How to do it...

1. Create a New Project by either clicking **File** and then **New Project**, or pressing *Ctrl+Shift+N* (shortcut).

2. In the **New Project** window, choose **Java Web** on the **Categories** side and **Web Application** on the **Projects**, then click **Next**.

3. At **Name and Location**, click on **Use Dedicated Folder for Storing Libraries**.

4. Now, either type the folder path or select one by clicking on **Browse**.

5. After choosing the folder enter **Project Name** as CreatingLibraries and, proceed by clicking **Next** and then **Finish**.

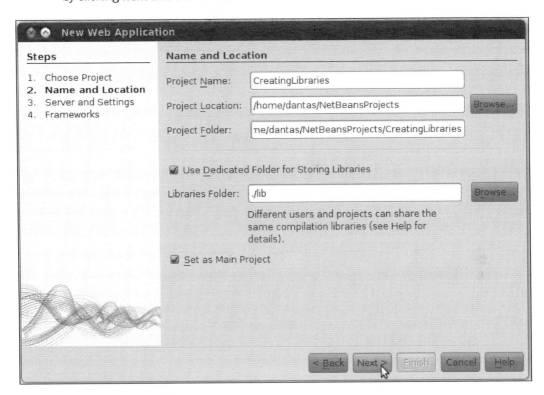

How it works...

Since we are creating libraries, a new project is going to be needed for this purpose. Projects can be packaged as libraries and reused in other projects to extend their functionality. Let's not worry about changing any of the default values that are set by the IDE for Project Name and web servers, since it is not a part of the scope of this recipe.

When selecting **Use Dedicated Folder for Storing Libraries**, it should be noted that this is where the libraries required for compilation will be stored.

NetBeans will perform the heavy lifting of copying all the necessary libraries to the specified folder. After following these steps, a new project will be created with the shared libraries folder at the chosen location.

There's more...

The usage of a Java Web project is just to exemplify; but projects in normal Java, Java ME, or Java EE would also follow these same steps with the same results.

If you are feeling curious, a good suggestion is to check the folder and file structure of the newly created `lib` folder.

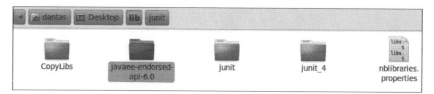

Sharing libraries

After creating a library directory, the next step is to actually share the project's library.

When projects become mature enough, or just for testing purposes, the developer can package the entire project into compressed Java Archive Files (JAR). These compressed files might be enterprise (EAR) or web (WAR) format, or simply JARs.

For this recipe, we will be using the previously created project and creating the WAR file from it.

Getting ready

If no Project is currently available at the **Projects** tab, follow the *Creating libraries* recipe to ensure that this recipe will work.

How to do it...

1. Click on the **Projects** tab, or press *Ctrl+1*.
2. Right-click on the project's name and click on **build**.

   Or

3. Click on **Files**, or press *Ctrl+2*, to navigate to the File structure of the project.
4. Expand the project node by double-clicking on the project's name.
5. Right-click on `build.xml`.
6. Select **Run Target**.
7. On **Run Target**'s sub menu, click on **dist**.
8. The **Output** panel will show the path in which the WAR file is placed.

How it works...

NetBeans uses Apache Ant as the automated building system of choice.

This script is incorporated into NetBeans menus while on the Projects panel, as seen by the build menu. By clicking on build, NetBeans will call the Ant script and initiate the process of bundling all the necessary files of this project into the WAR file.

The second step-by-step is given as an example on how to access the **dist** target through the Files panel.

There's more...

Unsure which way to execute? And why is it good to have a separate `build.xml` generated by NetBeans?

File Structure or Project Structure?

The second method, though longer, is very complete in the sense that other targets can be attained, in case the dist is not necessarily what we want.

What is the advantage of a separate ANT build file?

The advantage with NetBeans `build.xml` is that it can be used outside the IDE as well; very useful if you are deploying the application in a machine that does not have access to a Graphical Interface. It also lets the project be packaged without the necessity of using NetBeans.

For example, sometimes the developer needs to connect remotely to some server that does not provide a graphical window manager to solve issues/bugs/introduce features. In this case, it is easy to make necessary changes, package the solution, and deploy to the application server.

Importing Projects from Eclipse

If you wish to work alongside Eclipse or MyEclipse, NetBeans lets you use the Project Import functionality.

This functionality will import one or more projects created by the Eclipse IDE simply by specifying the workspace in which they are housed.

Getting ready

A valid Eclipse project, with sources and dependencies, must be used in order to continue with this recipe.

How to do it...

1. Click on **File** and then on **Import Project** and **Eclipse Project...**.

2. In the **Import Eclipse Project** window, select **Import Eclipse Project**.

3. Click on the **Browse...** button. An Open dialog will pop-up for workspace selection.

4. After selecting a valid workspace project, click the **Next >** button.

5. In the **Projects to Import** section, select the projects you want to import.

6. Select **Store NetBeans project data inside Eclipse project folders**.

7. Click the **Finish** button.

How it works...

By selecting the workspace directory, NetBeans will then analyze and convert the metadata created by Eclipse.

The project structure, along with the dependencies, will be available for NetBeans usage. It is important to notice that NetBeans will not change the way the Eclipse project behaves.

On **Store NetBeans project data inside Eclipse project folders**, NetBeans will create its own structure inside the Eclipse folder structure. Select this option if you want to distribute the NetBeans project directory in a Version Control System. This ensures that libraries and configuration files used by Eclipse and NetBeans are the same.

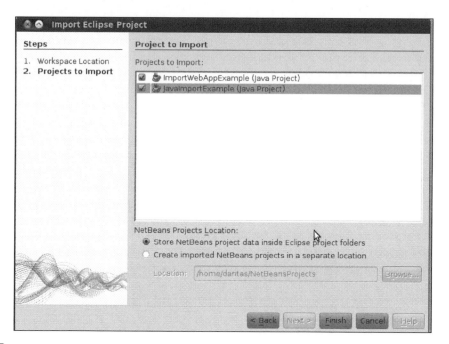

It is also possible to use NetBeans without placing its configuration files inside Eclipse's workspace. If this is the desired outcome, then select **Create imported NetBeans projects in a separate location** and then click on **Browse...** to select the folder where NetBeans configurations will exist.

The imported Eclipse projects will then be placed on the **Projects** tab on the right-hand side.

In the *There's more...* section, there is a list of some errors that might arise when importing an Eclipse project.

There's more...

Now let's talk about some other options, as well as some pieces of general information that are relevant to this task.

Synchronizing Eclipse

With multiple developers working on a project, it is common that changes to a project happen from time to time. When this happens, NetBeans can resynchronize the projects by the following:

- ▶ **File**
- ▶ **Import Eclipse Project**
- ▶ **Resynchronize Eclipse Projects**

After following these steps, the classpaths of all the projects imported to Eclipse will be in sync. Changes to your local project will not be synchronized back, however. This way, NetBeans ensures that the local configurations will not damage the parent project.

More error dialogs

While importing Eclipse projects, some importing errors might come up.

Many of these errors are not specific to our recipe but the following notes might come in handy while developing future projects.

Some of these errors are:

- ▶ **Resolve Missing Server Problem**: Just right-click on the project node and browse to the folder where the server is installed.
- ▶ **Resolve Reference Problem**: Occurs when libraries are missing from the project class path. Solving this is very similar to the missing server problem. Right-click on the project node and select **Resolve Reference Problem**, and then select the folder where the library is.

▶ **Eclipse platform for Project Name cannot be used. It is a JRE and the NetBeans project requires a JDK. NetBeans will use the default platform**: This is due to the Eclipse project being configured with a JRE instead of JDK. To solve this, click on the toolbar in **Tools**, and then select **Java Platforms**. The **Java Platform Manager** will be shown, click on **Add Platform...** and from the options, select the correct Java Platform the application is being developed on.

Importing existing Maven Projects

With NetBeans, Maven support is already integrated to the IDE. And with the latest release, 7.0, Maven 3.0 is integrated.

There is no requirement to download or configure plugins. It is as simple as that.

Getting ready

Note that even if Maven is not in the System Path, NetBeans already has an embedded version for ease of use. This is very useful if there is no specific Maven version to be used.

However, it is a good practice to install and configure Maven properly.

For more information, visit: `http://maven.apache.org/`.

An existing Maven project should exist in order to continue with this recipe.

How to do it...

To open a Maven project:

1. Click on **File** and then **Open Project** or press *Ctrl+Shift+O*.
2. The **Open Project** dialog will be shown.

Select the folder where the Maven project is placed by clicking on **Look In** (A Maven project will have the following icon):

Once the **File name** changes to the correct folder, click **Open Project**.

How it works...

NetBeans recognizes Maven projects based on the **Project Object Model** (**POM**) files and certain other characteristics intrinsic to the format.

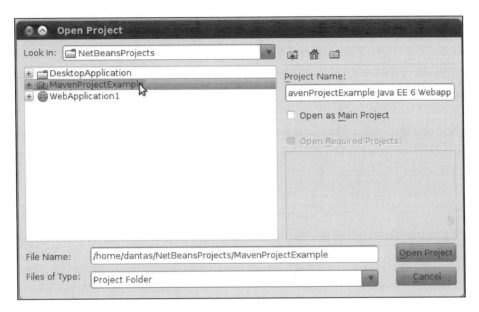

After clicking **Open Project**, the **Projects** tab will show the Maven structure.

Maven, like Ant, helps developers package and maintain projects. Developers can perform certain tasks by invoking Maven goals, such as packaging and executing test cases.

2
Basic IDE Usage

In this chapter, we will cover:

- ▶ Creating a Java Project using Maven support
- ▶ Creating a package
- ▶ Creating a class
- ▶ Running the main class
- ▶ Debugging a class
- ▶ Creating constructors
- ▶ Generating toString(), equals(), and hashCode()
- ▶ Generating getters and setters

Introduction

Now that we are all set, let's start with what every developer loves: coding.

NetBeans features a handful of project wizards. These wizards abstract the tedious job of creating folder structures and automate most of the job required by the developer in terms of importing the required libraries.

Creating a Java project with NetBeans Wizards is simple and easy. With NetBeans' help, we will explore the basics of project creation and configuration. Some more advanced project creations, like Maven support, are also covered in this chapter. These are actually the first steps of more advanced projects that will come in later chapters. Besides using Projects Wizards, this chapter shows the Java editor for the first time. As with other IDEs NetBeans also eases the creation of files such as: Classes, interfaces, JSP's, Servlets, and many more can be easily created with a few clicks.

Apart from the rich set of wizards, NetBeans features a great Java debugger and in this chapter you will learn how to debug a simple Java class.

Creating a Java Project using Maven support

Apache Maven is a build automation and project management tool hosted by the Apache foundation.

It uses a XML file called **Project Object Model file (POM)** to describe tasks, dependencies and goals that will be used to package, compile and even deploy out application in servers. Recently, Apache Maven has had a surge of interest since it has become an industry standard; it simplifies development, facilitates a test-driven approach, can be used for continuous integration, and simplifies cooperation between developers in a team who are working with different tools. For these reasons, the NetBeans team decided that the IDE should have built-in support for it. Since version 6.7, this is bundled together with the IDE, making the usage of Maven as easy as possible.

Maven can also be used by the command line, its primary usage, but a handful of commands must be memorized, such as package and clean. By using NetBeans instead, one can rely on a list of commands that are already pre-loaded with the IDE. This will ensure that the developer is just one click away from finding out the command that keeps on slipping their mind.

Getting ready

Maven is already built-in to the NetBeans IDE, but if you want to use Maven in your everyday work, you should also have Maven installed in your system. Although using the bundled Maven in NetBeans is not a good practice for production environments, it can be used as a temporary solution.

Apache Maven can be found at: `http://maven.apache.org`

The latest release of NetBeans supports Maven 3.0, which is also the latest release from Apache.

How to do it...

1. To create a New Project either click on **File** and then **New Project** or press *Ctrl+Shift+N*. On the **New Project** window, two panes will be shown. Choose **Maven** at the **Categories** side, **Java Application** on the **Projects** side, then click **Next**.

2. At the **Name and Location** step, **Project Name** should be filled with `HelloMaven`.

3. Leave all the other options, meaning: **Project Location**, **Group Id**, **Version**, and **Package**, with their default settings, and click **Finish**.

How it works...

The first time a Maven project is created with NetBeans, the IDE will automatically handle all Maven configurations and generate the necessary files for future project creations.

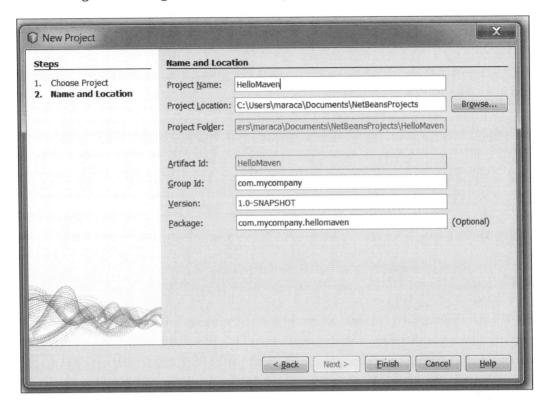

Maven archetypes are the models where projects are defined, maintained, and developed. Selecting the Maven Archetype will create a standard Java project. NetBeans will do the following (you can confirm this in the Project View):

1. Create the package structure.
2. Copy the necessary libraries to the **Libraries** folder.
3. Copy the necessary testing libraries to the **Test Libraries** folder.
4. Automatically generate a main class and place it under **Source Packages**.
5. Automatically generate a test class and place it under **Test packages**.
6. Place the POM file under **Project files**.

There's more...

Learn why the IDE needs to download a repository locally and how to edit the POM file.

Speeding Maven development

The IDE will also download a repository index from the central repository. This local index of the commonly-used archetypes will speed up the creation process when new archetypes are necessary.

Editing POM

Under the **Projects** tab, expand the **Project Files** node and double-click on `pom.xml`. This will open the XML editor, making it possible to edit this file. Feel free to explore what each tag means and edit it.

See also

For importing an existing Maven Project, try our *Importing existing Maven Projects* recipe in the *NetBeans Head First* chapter.

Creating a package

Everything is better when organized. With this in mind, we will check how to create packages using the IDE.

Besides being more organized, it is bad coding practice to leave all classes in the same package or in the root package.

How to do it...

First we will need to create a new project, so please refer to our recipe *Creating a Java Project using Wizard* in the beginning of this chapter, for project creation. When naming the project, enter `CreatingPackages`. When the **Projects** tab shows the **CreatingPackages** project, expand the **CreatingPackages** node, if not yet expanded.

Now we will create a package for our source code:

1. Expand the **Source Packages** node (if not yet expanded).
2. Right-click on **com.creatingpackages**.
3. Select **New** and then click on **Java Package...**.

4. In the **Package Name** text field, append `gui` (so that it looks like **com.creatingpackages.gui**).

5. Leave **Location** set as **Source Packages**.

6. Click **Finish**.

A new empty package will be shown right under **com.creatingpackages**.

And finally, a package for our unit test source code:

1. Expand the **Test Packages** node (if not yet expanded).

2. Right-click on **Test Packages**.

3. Select **New** and then click on **Java Package....**

4. In the **Package Name** text field, type **com.creatingpackages.tests.gui**.

5. Leave **Location** set as **Test Packages**.

6. Click **Finish**.

A new empty test package named **com.creatingpackages.tests.gui** is shown below **Test Packages**.

The final setup should look like this:

How it works...

Having understood that, we will see both ways of creating a package: one, by clicking on the desired folder destination, where the package will reside and the other, by clicking where the root node of the package will be.

By right-clicking on **com.creatingpackages**, the IDE will understand that we wish to create a package under the current one and will then automatically append the full path of the packages in Package Name. The user then needs to only type the rest of the path. This saves a lot of time when the project grows and nested packages start to spread.

The second option is to right-click directly on the desired node in the **Packages** tab. In our example we are creating a package under **Test Packages**. Right-clicking on the **Test Packages** node will trigger a clean Package Name and it is up to the developer to decide what the full path is going to be.

There's more...

It is also possible to create packages in the **Files** tab and with a new Class creation wizard.

The Files tab

By navigating to the **Files** tab, it is possible to see how the folder structure is organised, similarly to the **Projects** tab. It is also possible to create a Package using this view by following the same steps described previously.

The **Files** tab differs from the **Project** view in the sense that the files are presented as they exist in the filesystem. The **Project** view on the other hand, presents the files as they are organized from the project perspective.

Automatic creation of packages

It is also possible to create packages when a new class is created by the IDE.

Creating a class

One of the most repetitive tasks in software development is creating classes. Once again, with NetBeans wizards, creation of classes is very easy and straightforward.

Getting ready

It is necessary to have a project in order to create a class, so if you are unsure on how to do this, please check the *Creating a Java project using Wizard* recipe. However, when naming the project, enter `CreatingClasses`.

How to do it...

When the **Projects** tab shows the **CreatingClasses** project, expand the **CreatingClasses** node, if not yet expanded.

Even though NetBeans will create a main class, we will create another one:

1. Right-click on the **CreatingClasses** project, and select **New** and **Java Class...**.
2. On the **New Java Class** window, type **MyClass** under **Class Name**.
3. On the **package** selection, click on the dropdown and select **creatingclasses**.

4. Add **.my** as a suffix in the **Package**. This will be shown as **creatingclasses.my**.

5. Click **Finish**.

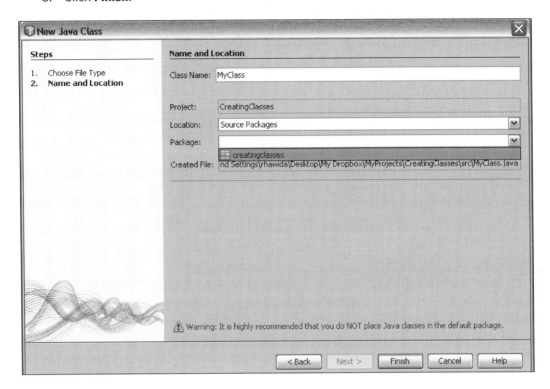

How it works...

The class is created relative to the path of the right-click. Having said that, this example shows that it is also possible to create packages during class creation.

By appending a dot (.) as a suffix, the IDE will create a Java class and a package. In this case, package `creatingclasses.my` and a class called MyClass.

The class created by the IDE is a very basic one. Added by the IDE are comments and package path, along with the class declaration.

There's more...

Discovering hidden file types with the Other option.

Other file types

Any number of files can be created by using this method. If curiosity strikes, check the files under **Other...** after right-clicking on a project name and selecting **New**.

Running the main class

It is possible to compile and run the main class straight from NetBeans IDE. The primary reason for executing the main class is fairly obvious, that is, to test that modifications made in the software are actually what the coder(s) intended.

How to do it...

It is necessary to have a project in order to create a class, so if you are unsure how to do this, please check the *Creating a Java project using Wizard* recipe. However, when naming the project, enter `RunMainClassApp`.

With the main class open, enter the following line of code inside of the `main()` method:

```
System.out.println("Main class output");
```

Then right-click inside the Java editor of the `Main.java` file and select **Run File**.

How it works...

NetBeans will always show the **Run File** option for a Java class that contains the main method.

After Run File is selected, NetBeans will then compile and execute it. The output, if any, of the main class will be shown in the Output view.

For this example, the output is: **Main class output**

There's more...

Thinking that using the mouse is overkill? Or prefer running the entire project?

Run class shortcut

It is much faster to use some key combinations than to reach for the mouse every time. So, if changes need to be checked fast, just hit *Shift+F6* and the class will be executed.

Run project shortcut

With a Java Desktop project there is a possibility to run the entire project. With this specific type of project, the Main class, the one created by NetBeans, is the one to execute.

It is possible to run the main project by right-clicking on the project name and selecting **Run** or pressing *F6*.

Debugging a class

It is possible to set breakpoints and watches in NetBeans and, on execution, check what the value of a given variable or object is.

NetBeans debugger also lets the developer follow method calls and execute code one line at a time giving a fine-grained visualization on how the code is running.

This is one of the features where NetBeans shines in comparison to other IDEs so without further ado, let's dive in. NetBeans has already included many of the plugins, performance tools, and servers that are used for easing the process of setup and debugging.

Getting ready

We will be using a Java Application Project for this example. Since we are just showcasing the capabilities of the debugger too, we won't be using anything complicated; a normal Java Application Project will suffice. If you're unsure on how to create one, please check the recipe *Creating a Java Project using Wizard*.

We are also going to need a Java class. If the *Creating a Java Project using Wizard* recipe was used, then a main class is already generated and that one can be used in our example. If a project already exists, then it is possible to follow the *Create a class* recipe in order to get a clean class for the work to proceed. The automatically generated class will be our main class, so the class name is `Main.java`.

If the *Creating a Java Project using Wizard* recipe is followed, the project name used for this recipe would be **HowToDebugApp** and all of the default settings present on the wizards should be left untouched.

How to do it...

We will need another class to demonstrate how to setup breakpoints in other objects.

1. Right-click on **Source Packages**, under the **HowToDebugApp** project, select **New** and **Java Class...**.
2. On the **New Java Class** window, type **Person** under **Class Name**.
3. On **package** selection, click on the dropdown and select **howtodebugapp**.
4. Click **Finish**.

The `Person.java` file will show up on the Java Editor.

Inside the Person class declaration, write:

```
int age;
String name;
```

Now lets refactor our class by encapsulating the fields:

1. Right-click on the `Person` class inside the Java Editor.

2. Select **Refactor** and then click on **Encapsulate Fields....**

3. Then click on **Select All** and **Refactor**. The getters and setters will be added to `Person.java` and the fields will have the visibility modifiers set to private.

4. Open `Main.java`. If `Main.java` is not open in the Java Editor, double-click it.

Inside the main method, enter the following:

```
Person person1 = new Person();
Person person2 = new Person();

person1.setName("Rhawi");
person1.setAge(28);
person2.setName(null);
person2.setAge(32);
```

It is not good practice to set variables with null values but, for the purpose of this example, we will do it this one time.

A watch is exactly what the name says, it "watches" a specific variable for the entire lifetime of the application and displays its value in the variables view.

To add a watch, simply:

1. Select `person1` variable.

2. There are two ways to add a watch: On the top bar, click on **Debug** and then **New Watch...** or press *Control+Shift+F7* and click **OK**. `person1` will be added to the **Variables** view.

For our first breakpoint, click on the left-side bar, where line numbers are placed, specifically on the line shown below:

```
person2.setName(null);
```

A breakpoint will be added to the side bar and a long pinkish line will specify the breakpoint location.

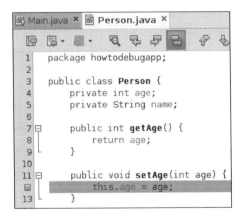

Then add another breakpoint, but this time to `Person.java`, where the line is:

```
this.age = age;
```

Finally, let's debug our example. Open `Main.java` and press *Control+Shift+F5*.

How it works...

Upon the debug mode execution, NetBeans stops the execution at the first breakpoint.

The breakpoint tells the IDE to temporarily halt the program and let the developer examine the contents of variables and watches at that point.

In our example, NetBeans will look like this:

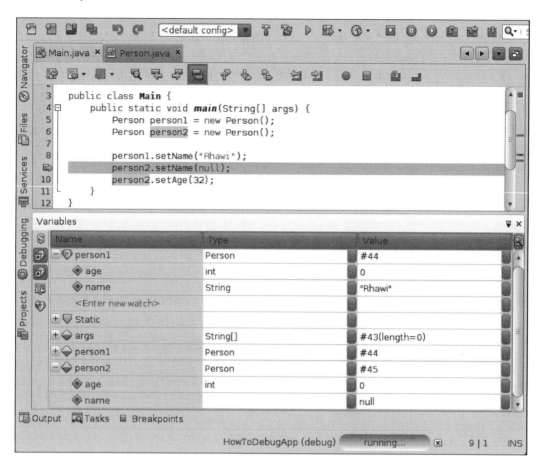

It is possible to see our watch, shown with a blue diamond icon, and also the normal variables, shown with a green lozenge. It is possible to expand the watch or variables to check the contents of the object on runtime.

The execution point is highlighted in green. To jump one line of code in the execution, press *F8*. To continue press *F5*; the IDE will resume the debugging process until another breakpoint is found, at which point the execution will once again stop, so that the developer can have another chance to examine the execution. In our example, the execution will continue until the Person's set method for age is reached. To continue with the execution, just press *F5* one more time and the program execution will continue until the end, since we do not have any other breakpoints.

To remove a breakpoint, simply click on it and it will disappear.

There's more...

What if I want a breakpoint when my variable reaches a certain value? Watches are too complicated, is there something easier? Does NetBeans debug other types of applications?

Conditional breakpoints

It is possible to create breakpoints with conditions.

Just right-click on the breakpoint, select **Breakpoint**, and then **Properties**. A **Breakpoint Properties** window will show up, with a section where the conditions can be specified.

Other ways to check variable content

It is also possible to check the contents of a variable without needing to watch the **Variables** view. When the execution stops, just place the mouse pointer over the variable. A tooltip will be shown with the variable result.

This is very fast and useful especially when you first start debugging, and don't know what watches are needed yet.

Different kinds of debuggable applications

In this recipe, we used a Java Desktop application as a base for our example. But debugging can also be used with different applications, such as Web Apps and Mobile Apps, which are also written in different programming languages.

Creating constructors

All classes have constructors, even if these constructors are just default ones. But what happens when the constructors starts to get bigger and bigger, and harder to maintain? With just two key strokes, we can automatically generate constructors for NetBeans.

Getting ready

Check the recipe *Creating a Java Project using Wizard*.

Feel free to modify the default settings, but if you wish to follow exactly what we are presenting here, just modify the Project Name to **CreatingConstructorsApp** and uncheck **create main class**.

How to do it...

With the project open:

1. Right-click on the **CreatingConstructorsApp** project and select **New** and **Java Class...**.

2. On the **New Java Class** window, type **Address** under **Class Name**.

3. Under **package**, type **myclasses**.

4. Click **Finish**.

5. When the Address Java Class opens, insert the following code:

```
int zipcode;
int number;
String street;
String city;
```

6. Then press *Alt+Insert*. A small pop-up will be shown with the title **Generate**.

Select the first option, which is named **Constructor...**, then select all four fields, and click on **Generate**.

How it works...

NetBeans recognizes the fields in the class and generates the constructor based on the fields that were selected.

As best practice, NetBeans names all the constructor fields the same way as the declared variables.

There's more...

What about default constructors? And how to generate multiple constructors?

Default constructor creation

It is also possible to generate default constructors, constructors without any fields, by using this same method.

Simply press *Alt+Insert* and upon field selection, leave them all unmarked, and click on **Generate**. A default constructor will then appear inside the class.

Generating toString(), equals(), and hashCode()

To generate `toString()`, `equals()`, and `hashCode()`, the process is almost the same as with the constructor. However, it is important to know when to implement those methods and when not to. For example, if overriden, equals and hashCode must be implemented using the same set of fields in the code. The equals method should be used when equality is required, where it would be necessary to compare different instances of the class. The basic implementation checks for identity, the same as using ==. The hashCode method exists for two reasons: one being efficiency, so objects can be used with collections that require a hash, such as HashSet and HashMap, and the other being conformity with equals. So, when an object is equal to the other, hashCodes of those two objects must also be identical.

Getting ready

Check the recipe *Creating a Java Project using Wizard*.

Feel free to modify the default settings, but if you wish to follow exactly what we are presenting here, just modify the Project Name to **CreatingToStringEqualsHashCodeApp** and uncheck **create main class**.

How to do it...

With the project open:

1. Right-click on the **CreatingToStringEqualsHashCodeApp** project and select **New** and **Java Class...**.
2. On the **New Java Class** window, type **Book** under **Class Name**.
3. Under **package**, type **myclasses**.
4. And click **Finish**.

In the class body, insert the following:

```
int isbn;
String name;
String author;
int price;
```

Let's first generate `toString()`:

1. Place the cursor before the closing bracket (}).
2. Press *Alt+Insert*.
3. Select **toString()....** With all the fields selected, press **Generate**.
4. NetBeans will then implement `toString` and place it inside the body of `Book.java`.

Now, for `equals()` and `hashCode()`:

1. Once again, place the cursor before the closing bracket (}).
2. Select **equals()** and **hashCode()....**
3. Press *Alt+Insert*.
4. Select **isbn**.
5. Click **Generate**.

After pressing **Generate**, it is possible to see hashCode implemented.

How it works...

Since `toString()` is a method which usually requires all the information from the implementing object, we added all the present fields to the implementation when we generated it.

The case is a bit different with ISBN, since it is already a unique number, and other fields like name or author do not satisfy the uniqueness condition, so it was the only one selected.

There's more...

Want to know more about hashCode and equals?

hashCode() and equals() rules

There are few rules related to the use of hashCode and equals that are worth checking but are beyond the scope of this recipe:

```
http://www.ibm.com/developerworks/java/library/j-jtp05273.html
```

Generating getters and setters

Finally, let's take a look at one of the more tedious tasks in Java: implementing the getters and setters for all the fields in our class. With a few fields, there is not much work to be done but with time, classes might grow in size and more fields usually means more getters/setters.

Thanks to NetBeans' refactoring capabilities, this is just as easy as pressing *Alt+Insert*. Seriously!

Getting ready

Check the recipe *Creating a Java Project using Wizard*.

Feel free to modify the default settings, but if you wish follow exactly what we are presenting here, just modify the Project Name to **CreatingGettersSettersApp** and uncheck **create main class**.

How to do it...

With the project open:

1. Right-click on the **CreatingGettersSettersApp** project and select **New** and **Java Class...**.

2. On the **New Java Class** window, type **Account** under **Class Name**.

3. Under **package**, type **myclasses**.

4. And click **Finish**.

Inside the body of Account.java, insert:

```
String firstName;
String lastName;
String maritalStatus;
int id;
int accountNumber;
long saldo;
boolean accountActive;
```

After the last line of code and before the closing bracket (}), place the cursor and:

1. Press *Alt+Insert*.

2. Select **Getter and setter...**.

3. Select the uppermost checkbox that says **Account**.

4. Click on **Generate**.

NetBeans will then create all the getters and setters for all of the fields that are present in `Account.java`.

There's more...

Are the getters and setters mandatory and is it possible to add those methods later in the game?

Addition of newer get/set methods

It is also possible to regenerate getters and setters if more fields are added to the class.

Try adding a few variables and perform the steps once again when needed.

Also, not all fields will need getters and/or setters, so use them wisely. Some frameworks rely heavily on the usage of get/set pairs, such as Spring and EJB.

3
Designing Desktop GUI Applications

In this chapter, we will cover:

- ▶ Creating a Java Desktop Application
- ▶ Creating a Frame
- ▶ Creating a Panel
- ▶ Adding Event Listeners
- ▶ Connecting your application to a database
- ▶ Creating a customized icon for your application
- ▶ Making executable Desktop Applications

Introduction

One of the greatest strengths of NetBeans is the powerful Swing GUI Builder.

It uses Java's Swing as the default framework and with it, it's possible to:

- ▶ Create and design complex GUI applications
- ▶ Drag-and-drop components from a palette component
- ▶ Design beautiful-looking applications
- ▶ Previewing the changes before compiling
- ▶ Possibility to bind data straight from the Database to your component

And it's possible to do much more.

Besides being totally free, the Swing GUI Builder lets the developer concentrate on coding.

To learn more about Swing development, you can refer the following book:

```
https://www.packtpub.com/netbeans-platform-6-9-developers-guide/book
```

Starting with the basics, we will see how to create a simple Java Desktop Application and then build on that by adding panels, GUI controls, and connections to databases.

Furthermore, we'll also cover details like customizing the icon of the applications and creating executables for easier distribution. This will give a more professional look to the applications.

Another great thing about the Swing GUI Builder is that it can be extended with other frameworks, and not just plain Swing. We will show you how to extend a default component palette with an additional SwingX widget.

For more details about SwingX, please visit:

```
https://swingx.dev.java.net/
```

In this recipe we will be using, as with throughout the entire book, the Java SDK 6 that can be found at:

```
http://www.oracle.com/technetwork/java/javase/downloads/index.html
```

and NetBeans Java version, since it will support Java SE, Platform, and bundled servers.

Creating a Java Desktop Application

In this recipe, you will see how to create a new Java Desktop Application project. You will have to understand the component Palette, which classes are created by the IDE and what they represent for your application, and how to use the inspector to see which components are in your project.

How to do it...

1. Create a Java Desktop Application project; this can be achieved by clicking **File** and then **New Project** or by pressing *Ctrl+Shift+N* (shortcut).

2. In the **New Project** window, choose **Java** on the **Categories** side, **Java Desktop Application** on the **Projects** side, then click **Next**.

3. A disclaimer window will be shown, click **Next**.

4. At **Name and Location**, click on **Project Name** and enter **DesktopApp**.

5. At **Choose Application Shell**, select **Basic Application**.

6. Tick the box on **Use Dedicated Folder for Storing Libraries**.

7. We can now proceed by clicking **Next** and then **Finish**.

The following screenshot shows how the third step of the wizard should look like:

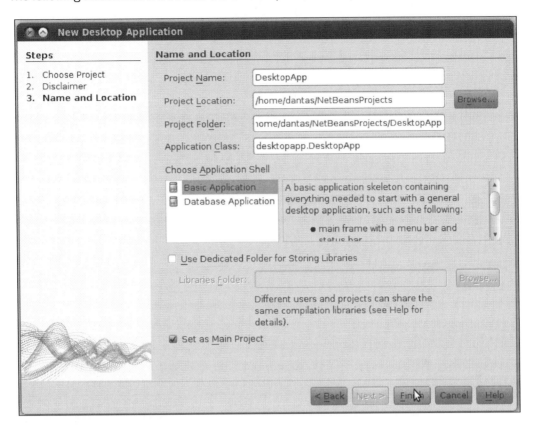

How it works...

Creating a Desktop application presents us with new options. The **Choose Application Shell** gives two:

▶ Basic Application

▶ Database Application

When one of these options is selected, NetBeans provides the user with some explanation of what files are being created and what to expect from them. This explanation can be seen at the right-hand side of the Application Shell. After following these steps, NetBeans will create a complete project structure that should look like this:

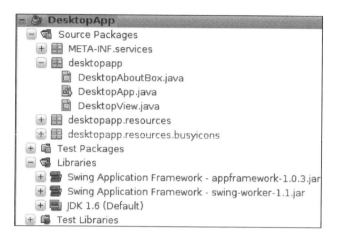

Three Java files are created as a skeleton, so that the developer can start coding on top of them to create an application. To create the applications, NetBeans follows the Swing Applications Framework. It is important to understand what each file does so we can implement them correctly:

 ▶ `DesktopAboutBox.java`: As seen in most Windows applications. It is implemented to give some information about the company, developer, and the version of application.

 ▶ `DesktopApp.java`: The application launcher. Basically it is used to initialize resources, inject them into the desktop app, and run the GUI class, in our case, DesktopView. This is where the main method exists.

 ▶ `DesktopView.java`: Our main graphical class. This is where we will lay out the components, program those components to react to events, and so on.

Note that these classes have different icons. `DesktopApp.java` has an icon corresponding to a normal Java class, since it is a normal Java class with a main method. The "Graphical" classes are seen with a representation of a small window inside the icon.

NetBeans creates these classes so it can better manage the design and placement of components in the Java files. This is achieved by the addition of a block of non-editable code, which is highlighted blue to differentiate it from the rest of the production code. This non-editable block is created by NetBeans as a blueprint for the entire application so the basic functionality will always be the same. If modification of this non-editable block were to be allowed, the application could perform in ways that could not be determined by the IDE.

It is possible to see this when toggling between **Design** and **Source** in the Java editor, as shown in the next screenshot:

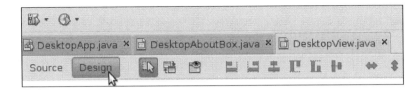

After selecting the design button, we have three small buttons available:

 Selection mode: Let's the developer choose the components that are inside the Form.

 Connection Mode: Launches a wizard that helps the developer to set an event that will establish a connection between objects.

 Preview Design: Launches a preview of the GUI that is being written.

The other subsequent buttons are used for component alignment and resizability.

By default, the main graphical class, in our case `DesktopView.java`, is already created with a few components:

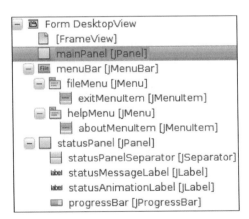

The components range from Panels and menus to a status bar. The component Tree View, in the previous screenshot, shows where each component belongs. In our case, Form DesktopView has a mainPanel [JPanel] and a menuBar [JMenuBar]. The menuBar then has a fileMenu [JMenu] and a helpMenu [JMenu], and so on. This kind of organization can have multiple levels in the hierarchy, and different components belonging to each level.

Form DesktopView is the main window where all of our components will be placed, or inside one of the child components.

From the component **Palette**, it is possible to drag-and-drop the components into **Form** under the GUI Designer.

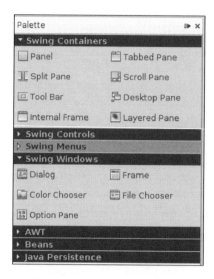

There are a number of toolkits available, such as Swing, AWT, and Persistence components. Each of these frameworks has its own separate tab. It is also possible to add components from external frameworks to our example, though we'll only use Swing Application Framework.

Under Palette, the **Properties** window displays **Properties**, **Binding**, **Events**, and **Code** related to the selected component in the **Designing** window:

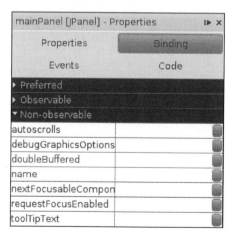

There's more...

Interested in seeing a cool Java Desktop project? It is not necessary to run the project to see the design changes in the application; check out how, in the following section.

Check the source for the Mars Rover Viewer

Of the sample projects available, the Mars Rover Viewer is the coolest and most complete Java Desktop Application, since it shows many concepts related to Swing Application Framework, background tasks, and resource maps, and is included with the IDE.

1. In the **New Project** window, expand **Samples** on the **Categories** side and select **Java** on the **Projects** side. Then select **Mars Rover Viewer** and click **Next**.

2. Leave all the default settings marked and then click **Finish**.

The contents of the Mars Rover Viewer will be shown in the Editor. After this, run the main project either by using the shortcut *F6* or by clicking on the **Run Main Project** button on the toolbar.

Preview Design

During development it is often neccessary, to check the behavior and design of the application. NetBeans grants a very convenient way to do this with the **Preview Design** button.

The launched window will present the coded events, like pressing a button to launch another window.

See also

This was just a general introduction on how to create Java Desktop Applications. So if you want to do something more productive with your application, it is recommended to please check the following recipes:

▶ Creating a Frame
▶ Creating a Panel
▶ Adding Event Listeners

Creating a Frame

NetBeans is using `javax.swing.JFrame` as a base for all Swing applications; in this recipe, we will use the word Frame to denote instances of `javax.swing.JFrame` class.

The Frame is nothing more than a border where the developer will place the components; think of a real frame where the canvas goes, so the artists can paint on it, and where other components will be added. The provided implementation from NetBeans is very basic in its content but it already has some basic controls, so the designer can close, expand, and align the components implemented.

Desktop Applications will have at least one Frame, but several other components can be included in its "body".

Getting ready

For this recipe, you will require a Java Desktop Project created according to the recipe *Creating a Java Desktop Application* recipe, given at the beginning of this chapter.

How to do it...

With the IDE and the Java Desktop Application project:

1. Right-click **desktopapp** package, select **New**, and click on **JFrame Form...**.
2. Under **Class Name**, write **MyJFrame** and click **Finish**.

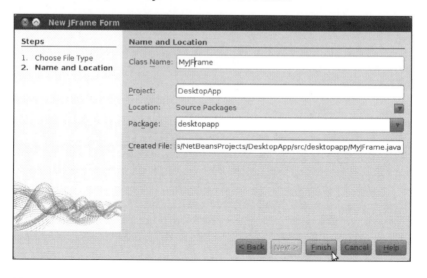

An empty JFrame will be shown on the editor.

How it works...

The IDE creates the `MyJFrame.java` class and places it under the `desktopapp` package. NetBeans then automatically generates the code for the default close operation, adds and configures a `javax.swing.GroupLayout`, and names it as "Form".

The execution behavior is also added by the IDE with a main method added to the body of the class, different from what was previously seen in *Creating a Java Desktop Application*.

So this is more of a "fresh start" for the entire application. No window, no status bar, and no other components. It is a clean sheet where the developers have total liberty to do what they want.

There's more...

Want to deploy your Swing application on a different platform from the one where it is being written? Want to check out what code was generated by NetBeans in the background? Your application does not need to close when pressing the **x** (close) button on the corner of the window.

Changing the look and feel of your application

Swing gives you the possibility of changing how your applications Look and Feel. The Look and Feel of an application is basically how the window border, buttons, titles, and system colors of a program are specified.

Swing has different Look and Feel for various operating systems, so your application will look different when launched under Windows, Linux, or Solaris.

To change the Look and Feel of you application:

1. Select **desktopapp** under the **Projects** window and right-click on it.
2. Then select **Properties**, expand the **Application** node, and select **Desktop App**.
3. Click on the drop-down named **Look & Feel** and select the desired one.

If you wish to check the look and feel of a configuration before setting it up as the default, then open the `MyJFrame.java` class and on the GUI Designer, click on **Design and the Inspector**. A window will appear on the left corner of the IDE.

Then right-click on the JFrame icon, select **Preview Design** and click on one of the three options given by the IDE: **Metal**, **CDE/Motif**, or **GTK+**.

On clicking the desired choice, the IDE will then launch the application with the modified Look and Feel.

NetBeans also gives users the option of downloading different Look and Feel files. Please visit the following links for more information:

`http://kenai.com/projects/nbsubstance/pages/Home`

`http://www.jtattoo.net/`

Checking the generated code

One of the main benefits in using the GUI Design is how practical and trivial it is to start your own application. If we check the contents of the files created by NetBeans, we can see how much heavy lifting the IDE does for us.

To check some of that heavy lifting, on the GUI Designer, click on **Source**; the IDE will then show the contents of `MyJFrame.java`.

Inside the editor, the code generated by the IDE is "hidden" from the user with an IDE configuration parameter.

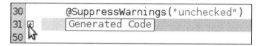

Expand the **Generated Code** and then the `initComponents` method to see the contents.

Where to find the default closing behavior

With the `MyJFrame.java` open and **Design** button toggled, check the properties window. The **Properties** button under **Properties** needs to be toggled.

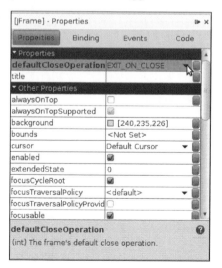

By clicking on the right-hand side of **defaultCloseOperation**, you'll get a drop-down menu with the following options:

- ▶ **HIDE**: Hides the window when clicking the exit button. It is possible to see whether the application is still running through the IDE.

- ▶ **EXIT_ON_CLOSE**: Closes the window when clicking the exit button. Similar to as if the window had called `System.exit(0)`.

- ▶ **DO_NOTHING**: No apparent response from the Frame.

- ▶ **DISPOSE**: Disposes (closes) the window. It behaves similarly to the **EXIT_ON_CLOSE** option when only one window is being used by that particular JVM.

Creating a Panel

In the next step, we will create a JPanel.

A JPanel can incorporate many different combinations of components and behaviors. This way, it is possible to interchange the Panels on top of the Frame and let other behavior take place at the window.

Each JPanel is configured with a layout; the layout determines how the components will be arranged on the top of the panel. NetBeans makes it easy to change the layouts with a click of a button.

Getting ready

It is necessary to have the source of a Java Desktop project open in NetBeans. Many of the files created in this recipe build upon previous recipes in this chapter, because we wish to give continuity to the recipes.

 If you are unsure how to do these steps, please refer to the previous recipes of this chapter.

The project and file name references come from the other recipes in this chapter, so feel free to use the same naming if not confident enough.

It is necessary to have an empty JFrame form so the JPanel can be used.

How to do it...

There are three ways to add a panel:

- ▶ Creating a new JPanel
- ▶ Drag-and-drop
- ▶ By Manipulating the JFrame

Below is the first method to create a new JPanel, we will call it Methood 1: Right-click on the package where the JPanel should be located and:

1. Select **New** and **JPanel Form....**A new window called **New JPanel Form** will be shown. In the Class Name field, type **MyJPanel**.

2. Leave all the other options as default and click on **Finish**.

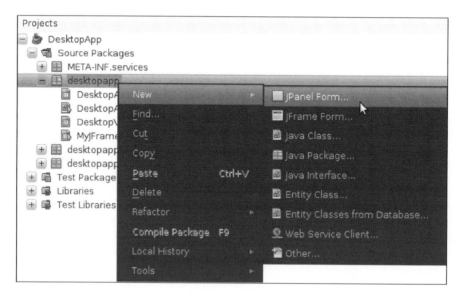

The MyJPanel.java class will be opened in the GUI Editor.

The Method 2 employes the drag-and-drop technique. In this method, we will use a JFrame created in the previous recipe.

Open `MyJFrame.java`, or some other JFrame implementation, so that the class will be shown in the GUI Editor:

1. With the **Palette** window open, expand **Swing Containers**.

2. Drag-and-drop the Panel icon into `MyJFrame.java`.

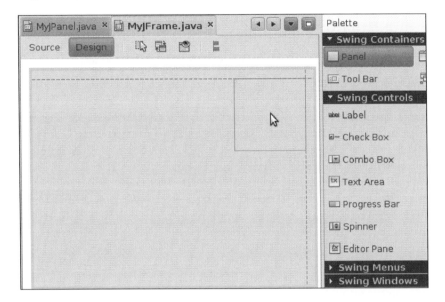

A component placing animation can be seen when the JPanel first enters `MyJFrame.java`. By clicking on a corner of the panel it is possible to resize the component.

Adding a Panel by right-clicking on the Frame (Method 3).

For method three, we will use a JFrame created in a previous recipe.

1. Open `MyJFrame.java`, or some other JFrame implementation. The class will be shown in the GUI Editor.

2. Right-click inside the `MyJFrame.java`.

3. Select **Add From Palette**, then select **Swing Containers**, and finally select **Panel**.

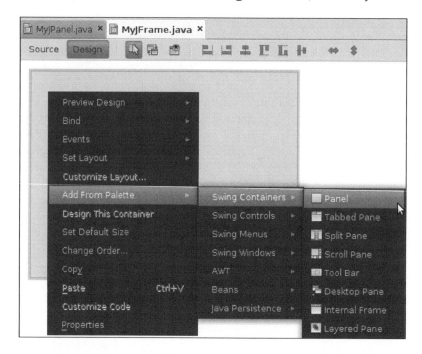

A centered panel in the middle of `MyJFrame.java` can be seen the the previous screenshot.

How it works...

All of the methods behave mostly in the same way, that is, they create a new Panel. The difference between method one and the others is that a new, separate class is created just for the Panel; while in the other ones, a Panel is inserted inside the JFrame implementation, applied to a Layout, and used from that. The choice between methods two and three is a matter of personal preference, since the IDE just adds and configures a JPanel.

There's more...

Interested in reusing JPanels as base implementations for bigger and more complex applications?

Reusing JPanels

Method one is especially useful if an application with different Panels is being built and these Panels are going to interact on top of some Frame.

How to do it: Right-click on the package where the JPanel should be located and:

1. Select **New** and **JPanel Form....** A new window called **New JPanel Form** will be shown.
2. Inside **Class Name**, type **MyBaseJPanel**.
3. Leave all the other options as default and click on **Finish**.

Let's design MyBaseJPanel with the components we think are proper for this base implementation.

Open `MyBaseJPanel.java` in the GUI editor and drag-and-drop the following components from the Palettes Swing Controls submenu:

- ▶ 5 Labels
- ▶ 1 Tree
- ▶ 3 TextFields
- ▶ 1 Button
- ▶ 2 Radio buttons

Arrange the components as you wish and then save the file.

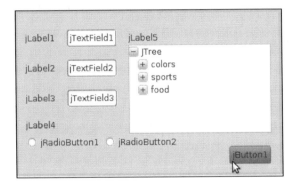

Open `MyJFrame.java` in the GUI editor and click on the corner of the Frame to resize it, making it bigger so the Panel can be accommodated inside the Frame, and finally drag-and-drop the MyBaseJPanel from the Projects window into MyJFrame.

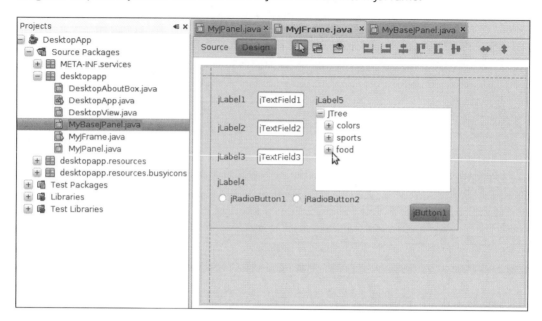

While placing the Panel inside the Frame, you may notice that the Panel does not occupy the entire area of the Frame. It is possible to select the Panel that was included by just clicking on the area where the Panel was dropped. You can use this to quickly select Panels for deletion.

Editing text label of components

There are two ways of changing the caption of the components:

1. By selecting the desired component and pressing F2. The component will then change its looks and let the user type the content.

2. By right-clicking on the component. After right-clicking on the component, select the first option, **Edit Text**, as shown in the following screenshot:

After making a few changes in the captions, it is possible to create an interface like this:

Adding Event Listeners

The next step after designing and building a Desktop application is to add behaviors to it.

In Swing, this is done by implementing Event Listeners. Swing Components register specific objects, the Event Listeners, in order to perform a determined task. When an event is triggered, the Listeners capture this call and handle the action according to what was implemented. Listeners also provide Events to those methods.

There are multiple kinds of events in Swing that range from mouse, focus, key, and window events.

For a more detailed view of Event Listeners, visit:

`http://download.oracle.com/javase/tutorial/uiswing/events/intro.html`

Getting ready

It is necessary to have the sources of a Java Desktop Application recipe in your NetBeans project folder. Many of the files created in this recipe build upon previous recipes in this chapter, because we wish to give continuity to the recipes.

> If you are unsure how to do these steps, please refer to the previous recipes in this chapter. The project and file name references come from the other recipes in this chapter, so feel free to use the same naming if you're not feeling confident.

The previous recipes *Creating a Panel* and *Creating a Frame* would be of great help in understanding why the design and components listed here are presented in this manner.

How to do it...

Open `MyBaseJPanel.java` in the GUI Editor with the Design mode selected.

To add an Event Listener:

1. Right-click on the **Clear...** button and select **events**, **mouse**, and then click on **mouseClicked**.

2. The Java editor will open up in Source mode. Inside the method, replace the TODO comment in `jButton1MouseClicked` with the following code:

   ```
   jTextField1.setText("");
   jTextField2.setText(«»);
   jTextField3.setText(«»);
   ```

3. Save the file.

4. Then add `MyBaseJPanel.java` to `MyJFrame.java`, if MyJFrame already contains MyBaseJPanel, then remove it, and press *Shift+F6*(shortcut).

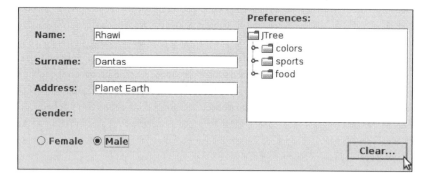

Now it is possible to write and clear the text that was placed inside the TextFields.

How it works...

When the sub-menu entry, the `mouseClicked` event is selected, NetBeans adds a mouse listener implementation to the `jButton1` object.

This can be seen by expanding the IDE-generated code block in the IDE. It is not possible to edit this code directly, since it is auto-generated by NetBeans. Changes to the implementation must be done from within the **Properties** window.

This is the relevant part of the IDE-generated code:

```
jButton1.addMouseListener(new java.awt.event.MouseAdapter() {
    public void mouseClicked(java.awt.event.MouseEvent evt) {
        jButton1MouseClicked(evt);
    }
});
```

The `MouseAdapter` is the interface used by the triggered event when a mouse is clicked. There are multiple methods in the `MouseAdapter` but we chose `mouseClicked` for this example.

NetBeans then adds a method, the `jButton1MouseClicked` method, with an empty implementation so the developer can add a behavior to it. In our case, we change the values of the Text Fields to empty Strings, clearing out their content.

There's more...

Unsure how to edit the code generated by the IDE?

Components Properties Window

Every component has properties and all of those properties can be edited directly using the **NetBeans Properties** window.

Placed on the left-hand side of the editor, this window will become available whenever a component is selected and will list the available options for that component.

Some of the options available in the **Properties** window are:

- ▶ **Properties**: Related to properties of the component, such as name, color, position, alignment, icon, and other configurations.

- ▶ **Binding**: Binds Components; for example, if you wish to update the progress of a status bar on a label, it is possible to do this by binding the components together. It's also possible to bind components with information held in a database or JavaBeans.

- ▶ **Events**: An alternative way of adding events instead of right-clicking on the component. Click on the drop-down menu and NetBeans will suggest a name for a method. If the suggested name is selected, NetBeans will change the view into Design mode, place the cursor inside the selected method, and enter the developer code.

▶ **Code**: Here it is possible to insert code inside the NetBeans-generated block. This is achieved by using the Pre and Post combination of various factors, such as Pre-init, Post-Listener, and Pre-adding. We can also configure other variable-related properties like visibility and name of the variable.

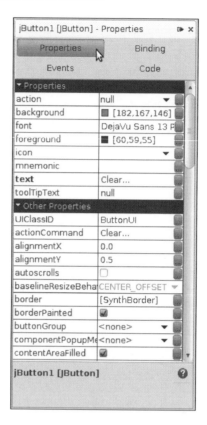

It is also possible to access the properties window by right-clicking on the component one wishes to know about and selecting **properties**. A new pop-up will be launched by NetBeans with the same contents as in the screenshot above.

Connecting your Application to a Database

Creating a Java Desktop application that communicates with a database using NetBeans is a breeze.

From the **Project wizard**, it is possible to create a basic GUI with the Create, Retrieve, Update, Delete (or CRUD) functionality that accesses a database.

The creation of such an application is simplified by the fact that NetBeans supports, out of the box, both **Java Persistence API (JPA)** and Beans Binding, besides supporting the Swing Application Framework as well.

The Java SDK 6 and GlassFish Server come bundled with a lightweight database, Java DB, which is a rebranded version of Apache Derby. Our recipes will be using Java DB since it's already bundled with JDK and is registered by NetBeans Services (so long as the chosen NetBeans installation package has Glassfish Server included). It is also possible to configure other Databases with NetBeans, which will cover in later chapters.

Java DB is not intended for production applications, which require databases with more features. For our purposes, however, the Java DB will more than suffice.

If you wish to learn more, please refer to:

- JPA: `http://www.jcp.org/en/jsr/detail?id=317`
- Java DB: `http://www.oracle.com/technetwork/java/javadb/overview/index.html`
- Beans Binding and Swing Application Frameworks: `http://blogs.sun.com/TechDaysEvents/entry/swing_application_framework_and_beans`

Getting ready

If another version of NetBeans is downloaded, one without GlassFish Server, the Java SDK version 6 comes with Java DB bundled.

Find the Java SDK 6 on:

`http://www.oracle.com/technetwork/java/javase/downloads/index.html`

If GlassFish is already installed, then Java DB will be detected by NetBeans and it will be automatically configured. If that is not the case, it is necessary to manually download, install, and register it.

How to do it...

Follow the next steps to create the database-ready Java Desktop Application:

1. Navigate to the Projects window.
2. Either right-click on the window and select **New Project...** or use the shortcut *Ctrl+Shift+N*.
3. On the right side of the **New Project** window under **Categories**, select **Java**.
4. In the same window, but under **Projects:** select **Java Desktop Application**.

5. Click **Next**, and **Next** again after the disclaimer.

6. When the third step, **Name and Location**, is reached under **Project Name**, type **DesktopApplicationDB**.

7. For the other fields, **Project Location**, **Project Folder**, and **Application Class**, leave the default information.

8. Under **Choose Application Shell**, select **Database Application**.

Upon making this selection, two more steps are added that are database-specific. The following screenshot shows what the screen should look like then:

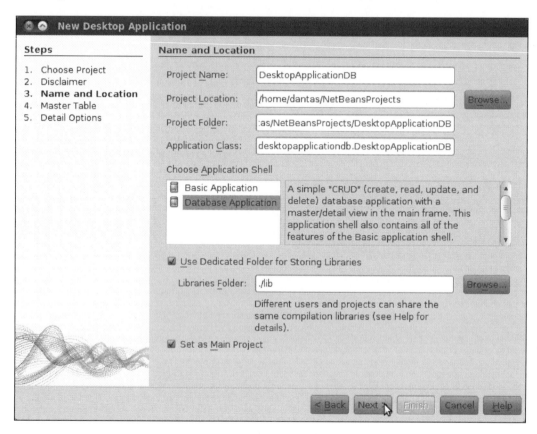

After the selection of the Database Application:

1. Click **Next >**.

2. Under **Database Connection**, select the **Java DB Sample APP**.

3. Under **Database Table**, select **CUSTOMER**.

4. Then on the left-hand side, on **Columns to Include**, select all of the following (to select multiple fields press and hold *Ctrl* while selecting them with the mouse):

   ❑ **CUSTOMER_ID**

   ❑ **NAME**

   ❑ **ADDRESSLINE1**

   ❑ **PHONE**

   ❑ **EMAIL**

   ❑ **CREDIT_LIMIT**

5. Press **<** to send all the selected fields to **Available Columns**.

6. Then Press **Next**.

7. On the **Detail Options**, under **Create Details Area As**, select **Text Fields**.

8. Click **Finish**.

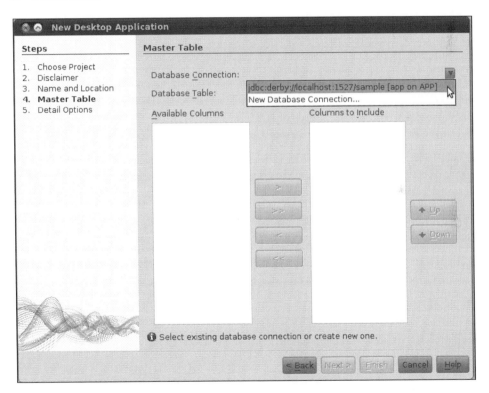

When the configuration of the Java Desktop Database Application is complete, it is possible to execute the project either by pressing *F6,* or by right-clicking on the project and selecting **Run**.

How it works...

The project creation and database configuration are pretty straightforward steps. At this point, the IDE is not doing anything different from a normal Java Desktop Project.

The JPA magic starts when selecting the table columns that are going to be included in the GUI. NetBeans then creates an entity class, `Customer.java` in our case, which is used to map the contents from the database to the GUI. The `persistence.xml` file, under the META-INF package, is used to configure the database connection and is tied to the Customer entity class.

The generated table is rendered in Swing and populated with content from the database, thanks to Bean Binding.

NetBeans generates code in the GUI class which makes it possible to edit the fields, save and delete information from the database, and refresh it.

Some of these methods are:

- ▶ `newRecord()`
- ▶ `deleteRecord()`
- ▶ `refresh()`
- ▶ `isSaveNeeded()`
- ▶ `setSaveNeeded(boolean)`

There's more...

Now let's talk about some other options, as well as some general information that may be useful for this task.

Registering a new database

If you wish to register a new database, (it is also possible to register other Databases besides Java DB), the next steps must be followed:

1. Select the Services window.

2. Right-click on **Databases** and select **New Connection...**.

3. In the **New Database Connection** window, under **Driver Name**, select the available driver or search for a new driver for your choice of database.

4. Fill the rest of the information related to the configuration of your database.

After entering all the required information and following the given steps, a new database will be registered.

Checking the contents of Customer.java

It is worth taking a look at the `Customer.java` entity class in order to understand the work that the IDE performs.

The IDE automatically creates SQL queries, adds support for updating (when the values of the query are edited in the GUI), adds and removes listeners, implements hashCode and equals methods, and more.

Looking even further, in `DesktopApplicationDBView.java`, it is possible to discover more code that is not present in a normal Java Desktop Application.

Using the Inspector to check for Binding

Wondering how Bean Binding is working together with the Swing components?

1. Select `DesktopApplicationDBView.java` and change to **Design** mode.

2. Expand the nodes Form DesktopApplicationDBView, mainPanel, masterScrollPane, and then right-click on **masterTable** and select **Properties**.

3. In **Properties** window, click on **Binding**.

4. Expand the Preferred option.

5. Inside the elements box list, click on the **...** box.

6. A **Bind masterTable.elements** window pops up.

This window will let you further configure the contents of the Binding.

Creating a customized icon for your application

One of the ways to customize your Java Desktop application and give it a more professional look is by adding an icon to it.

The icon will be used when the application is running, displayed in places like the task bar or when the user switches the application and the icons are displayed on the tab-switch.

Getting ready

For the purposes of this recipe, we will use an image in PNG format.

The image we will use for this recipe is the following:

It is necessary to have the sources of a Java Desktop recipe in your NetBeans project folder. Many of the files created in this recipe are a result of the previous recipes in this chapter being followed. This is because we wish to give continuity to the recipes.

How to do it...

With a Java Desktop Database Application open in NetBeans:

1. Open `DesktopApplicationDBView.java` and then navigate to the **Source** mode.
2. Inside the constructor, type:

   ```
   public DesktopApplicationDBView(SingleFrameApplication app)
   ```

   Find the following line of code with the ResourceMap:

   ```
   ResourceMap resourceMap = getResourceMap();
   ```

   And right after that line write:

   ```
   JFrame frame = getFrame();
   Image image = resourceMap.getImageIcon(«window.icon»).getImage();
   frame.setIconImage(image);
   ```

3. Then navigate to `desktopapplicationdb.resources` and open **DesktopApplicationDB.properties**.
4. On the last line of the properties file, add:

   ```
   window.icon=/images/green-v-icon.png
   ```

5. Finally, to add the icon image we need:
   - ❑ Create a folder: Under `<USER>/NetBeansProjects/DesktopApplicationDB/src` folder, create `USER>/NetBeansProjects/DesktopApplicationDB/src/images`.
   - ❑ Rename the application icon to: **green-v-icon.png**.
   - ❑ Then add the image to: `<USER>/NetBeansProjects/DesktopApplicationDB/src/images` with the name **green-v-icon.png**.

So the entire path needs to be:

<USER>/NetBeansProjects/DesktopApplicationDB/src/images/green-v-icon.png

Since we are using a database application for this example, the database, Java DB in our case, must be up and running. Here is how to connect to the database if unsure:

1. Navigate to the **Services** window.
2. Expand the **Databases** node.
3. On **jdbc:derby://localhost:1527/sample [app on APP]**, right-click and select **Connect...**.
4. Press *F6* to run the project and check if the icon is shown, for instance by pressing *Alt+Tab*.

In the Linux task switcher, it is shown like this:

Database Application Example

How it works...

We are loading the icon into the application from the constructor. For this, we are using the **ResourceMap**. It reads the parameters set inside **DesktopApplicationDB.properties**.

The ResourceMap is a holder that contains all the resources from our resource bundle, the `DesktopAapplicationDB.properties`. When instantiated, the ResourceMap returns values according to the keys being pressed.

This is a good approach since we are not hard-coding the path of the icon directly in the code and means the icon, or other properties as well, can be changed with minimal work.

There's more...

And what about a splash screen?

Adding a Splash screen

A splash screen is the screen that appears for a moment when the program is loading to tell the user that its execution has started.

For this example, we will use the same project we have used in this recipe, the **DesktopApplicationDB**.

For this to work, a splash screen image and the Java DB Sample App database must be up and running. If unsure how to do this, take a look at the *How to do it...* section of this recipe.

With the **DesktopApplicationDB** open in NetBeans projects window:

1. Right-click on the **DesktopApplicationDB** node and select **Properties**.
2. Navigate to **Application** and under **splash screen**, either click on **Browse...** or enter the path for the file.
3. Click **OK**.

And your application will have a working splash screen.

 Note that splash screens do not normally display when a project is being executed from within the IDE. It is necessary to navigate, with the command line, to the dist directory under your application's project path, in this recipe's case: `NetBeansProjects/DatabaseApplicationDB/dist`, and execute the following command:

```
java -jar DesktopApplicationDB.jar
```

Application startup and splash screen shown from a Linux shell:

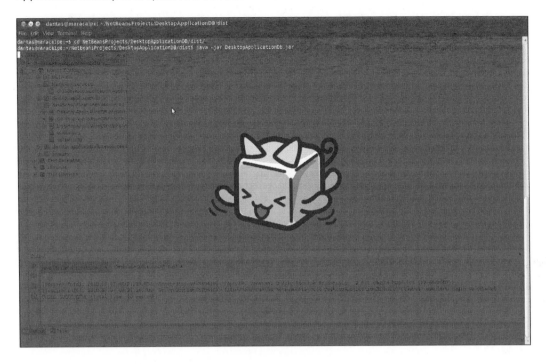

Application Properties and About box

The About box of an application gives the user useful information on where to find the application's main homepage, vendor's name, and other tidbits.

If you wish to quickly edit this without messing with the Swing components in the Design editor, here is how to do it:

1. With **DesktopApplicationDB** open under the **Projects** window, right-click on **DesktopApplicationDB** and select **Properties**.

2. Click on **Application** and fill the form with the desired information.

3. Click **OK**.

The **Common Application Properties** might look like this:

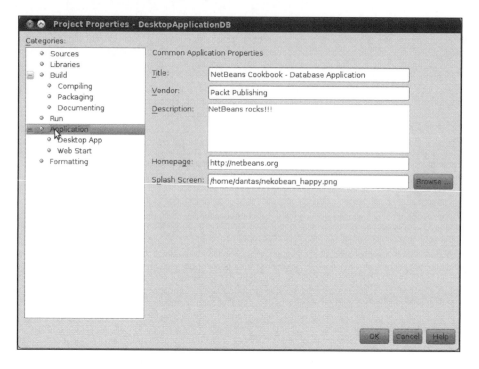

To view the changes, press *F6* or click on the **Run Main Project** button.

When the Application is shown, click on **Help** and then **About....**.

This is what the output looks like when the above information is entered:

Making executable Java Desktop Applications

After creating a Java Desktop Application, adding Frames and Containers, adding event listeners, and customizing the application, the only thing left is creating an executable. And making a lot of money (of course!).

Getting ready

It is necessary to have the sources of a *Java Desktop Database Application* in your NetBeans project folder.

It is necessary to have Java DB up and running. If unsure how to do this, please refer to *Chapter 4, Setting up Apache Derby/Java DB*.

The recipe, *Creating a Java Desktop Database Application*, would be of great help in understanding why the design and components listed here are presented in this manner.

How to do it...

With the Java Desktop Database Application open:

1. Right-click on the project name, in our case **DesktopApplicationDB**, and select **Properties**.
2. Click on **Libraries** and select the **Run** tab.
3. Click on the **Add Library...** button.
4. Add the following libraries: **Beans Binding**, **Swing Application Framework**, and **TopLink Essentials**, then click **Add Library**.
5. Then click **OK**.

6. Again, right-click on the project name, **DesktopApplicationDB**, and select **Clean and Build**.

The **output** window will show the path in which the JAR file was placed.

To distribute the application, simply compress the application in the desired format - ZIP and RAR are the most popular - and distribute it.

How it works...

When the Clean and Build task is executed, NetBeans generates the JAR file and automatically copies all the necessary libraries to the `lib` folder.

Here is a list of the libraries contained in `lib` folder, as shown in the next screenshot:

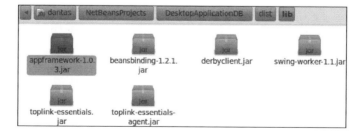

There's more...

How to execute and view the contents of JAR files.

Executing the JAR file

The IDE already gives, through the output window, all the required information to perform this task, but in case you missed it, here it goes:

Under Linux:

```
java -jar "<USER_DIRECTORY>/NetBeansProjects/DesktopApplicationDB/dist/
DesktopApplicationDB.jar"
```

Under Windows:

The same java -jar command from Linux can be used, pay attention to the different file delimiter present in windows.

Contents of the JAR file

Inside the JAR file, you will find that much of the work that the developer was once required to execute manually is now handled by the IDE.

Folder structure of the JAR file is as follows:

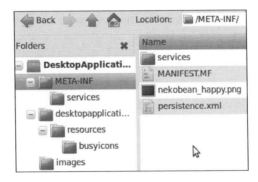

4
JDBC and NetBeans

In this chapter, we will cover:

- ▶ Setting up with MySQL
- ▶ Setting up with PostgreSQL
- ▶ Setting up with Apache Derby/Java DB
- ▶ Setting up with Oracle
- ▶ Setting up with Microsoft Access
- ▶ The built-in SQL editor

Introduction

NetBeans provides a great deal of integration with different services including databases.

It is possible to configure the IDE to work with commercial and open source Databases; even competing products from other vendors come integrated with NetBeans out-of-the-box.

With the built-in SQL editor and SQL Explorer NetBeans, your basic SQL needs will be satisfied.

Going further, NetBeans itself comes with bundled drivers for both MySQL and PostgreSQL. If you wish to use Java DB during pre-production, or just a lightweight database is needed, configuring it with NetBeans is very easy. The driver for Java DB comes bundled with both GlassFish server and Java SDK 6.

However, let's not forget that it is also possible to configure the IDE with support for other drivers. In this chapter, we will configure NetBeans with Oracle Corporation Databases and Microsoft Access. This can be done by finding the vender-supplied JDBC driver.

Forget third-party tools, forget over complicated configurations. It is that easy.

It doesn't stop there either. NetBeans provides database integration with different development frameworks, such as JSF, Swing Application Framework, and JPA.

Setting up with MySQL

MySQL is an Oracle Corporation product, was previously a Sun Microsystems one, and a MySQL Abs one before that. It is one of the most famous open-source relational database management systems, RDBMS, in the world. The code is available under the GNU license.

It is used by many companies, such as Nokia, Facebook, and Google, for its robustness and for being free for use.

At some point, Sun distributed installation packages of NetBeans bundled with MySQL, which is not the case anymore, but MySQL is still integrated and easily configured from it.

Getting ready

For this recipe we will use MySQL version 5.4.1 and MySQL GUI Tools.

Installation and configuration of MySQL Server and components onto the Operating System is beyond the scope of this recipe. What will be learned here is how to configure MySQL with NetBeans so that the integration between database and IDE can be achieved.

In this recipe, we assume that the Database is installed locally and the password is chosen by the user.

> For more information and downloads, visit the following link for the database:
> `http://www.mysql.com/downloads/mysql/`
> And for workbench visit `http://www.mysql.com/downloads/workbench/`.

How to do it...

With the IDE open:

1. Navigate to the **Services** window and expand the **Databases** section.

2. Right-click on Databases and select **Register MySQL Server...**.

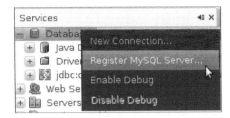

❑ A **MySQL Server Properties** window is shown.

4. Under **Basic Properties**, the IDE, by default, enters **localhost** as **Server Host Name** and **3306** as **Server Port Number**.

5. Then just add the **Administrator User Name** and **Administrator Password** that you configured during MySQL installation.

The MySQL Server Properties window should look more or less like this:

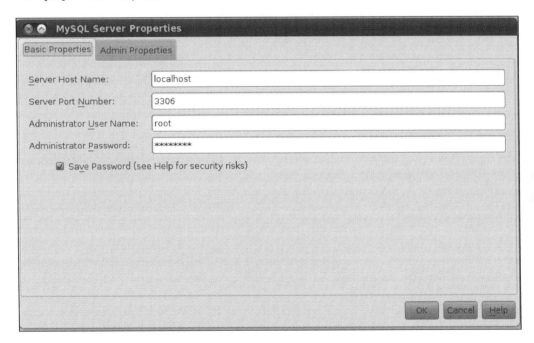

Then click on the **Admin Properties** tab. Under **Path/URL to admin tool**, enter the folder for the Administration tool and also the paths to start and stop commands for MySQL under shell or command prompt.

Then click **OK**.

An example of configured **Admin Properties**:

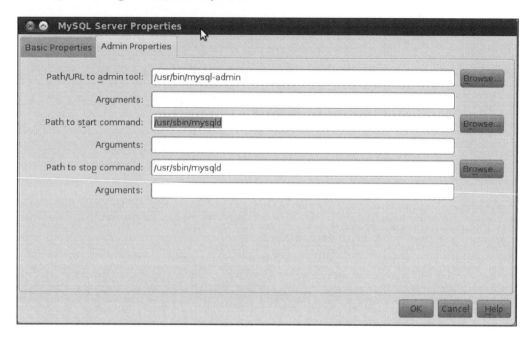

A MySQL node is added to the **Database** section of the **Services** window.

How it works...

The **Basic Properties** tab is the minimum information required to a connect to MySQL server this is all that is needed for the connection to work. The information required to better control the MySQL Server is on the **Admin Properties** tab. The Start and Stop commands and path for MySQL-related tools are also included in the submenu, which can be accessed by right-clicking.

Upon registration, there are two ways of checking whether MySQL Server is connected or not:

▶ If the **MySQL Server** node can be expanded, it means that it is connected

▶ The same node shows a `Not Connected` string

Once the node is expanded, the IDE will show the databases included in your server. Note that the number of databases included might differ from system to system, and if the MySQL Server already contains other databases.

There's more...

Want to Create Databases and Run the Administration tool from within the IDE? You've come to the right place.

Creating Databases

To create databases on a registered MySQL Server instance simply:

1. Right-click on the **MySQL Server at localhost** node and select **Create Database....**

2. A **Create MySQL Database** window will ask for **the New Database Name**. Enter `mysqltest` and press **OK**.

3. The **Databases** subsection will look like this:

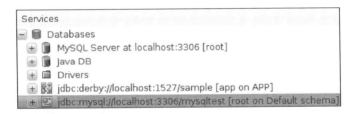

Running the Administration Tool

To run the MySQL Administration Tool, it is necessary to configure the IDE with the correct path. If unsure how to do this, refer to the beginning of this recipe, under **MySQL Server Properties**, in the **Admin properties** tab.

With the configuration in place:

1. Navigate to the **Services** window and expand the **Databases** node.

2. Then right-click on **MySQL Server at localhost**.

3. Select **Run Administration tool**.

Setting up with PostgreSQL

PostgreSQL is an object-relational database system, ORDBS, cross platform, and like MySQL, is also open-source and free. It is supported by a consortium of companies and names like Red Hat, Skype, and HP listed at their website.

As with MySQL, PostgreSQL also features a GUI for management called PGAdmin.

Setting up PostgreSQL with NetBeans is not as straightforward as with MySQL, but NetBeans still comes with the appropriate JDBC driver, so don't worry, it is still no rocket science.

Getting ready

For this recipe, we will use PostgreSQL version 8.4.4 and PGAdmin version 3.

Installation and configuration of PostgreSQL and components onto the Operating System is beyond the scope of this recipe. What will be learned here is how to configure PostgreSQL with NetBeans so that integration between the database and the IDE can be achieved.

In this recipe, we assume that the Database is installed locally and that the password is chosen by the user.

It is necessary to have an existing database in PostgreSQL for this recipe to work; we will assume that the name of the database is **mydb**.

How to do it...

With the IDE open, and PostgreSQL running:

1. Navigate to the **Services** window, right-click on the **Databases** node, and select **New Connection...**. When the **New Connection Wizard** window opens, select **PostgreSQL** from the dropdown menu, click **Next >** and enter the following information:
   - ❑ **Host**: 127.0.0.1
   - ❑ **Port**: 5432
   - ❑ **Database**: mydb
   - ❑ **User Name**: postgres
   - ❑ **Password**: postgres
   - ❑ Select the **Show JDBC URL** checkbox

2. The **Basic setting** tab should look like this:

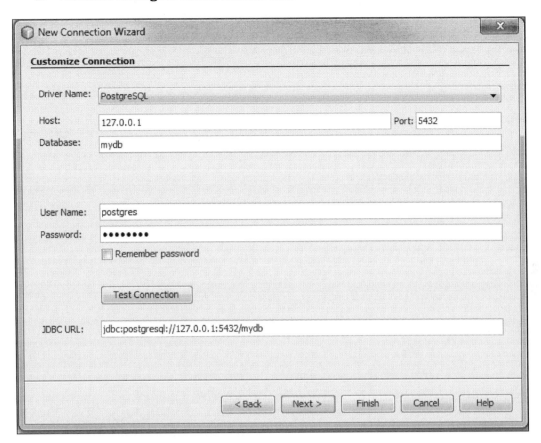

3. Click on **Finish**.

4. On the **Advanced** tab, click on the **Select Schema** drop-down and choose **public**, and then click **OK**.

5. A PostgreSQL connection node is added to **Databases**.

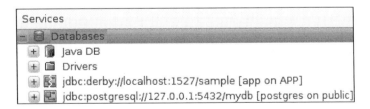

How it works...

NetBeans validates the entered information to access the database. This ensures that no misconfigured database is going to be used and prevents the user to actually create a a misconfigured connection and even prevents the user to proceed further in the wizard.

When Finish is clicked, NetBeans then connects to the PostgreSQL and fetches existing databases from the server. A new Database connection is placed under the **Databases** subsection of the **Services** tab.

There's more...

How to connect and disconnect PostgreSQL from within NetBeans?

Connecting and disconnecting

It is possible to connect to and disconnect from a database using the **Services** window.

Simply right-click on the desired connection and select **Connect...**, in case the database is disconnected, or **Disconnect**, if it is connected.

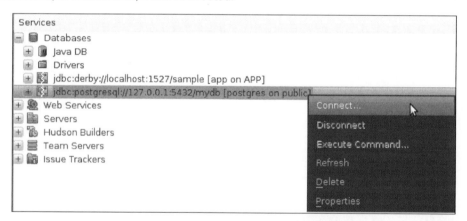

Setting up with Apache Derby/Java DB

Apache Derby is an Apache Foundation project that distributes an open-source RDBMS, with a staggering small footprint of only 2.6 MB, implemented in Java and is fully compatible with JDBC and SQL standards.

Java DB is Apache Derby, but packaged and distributed by Sun Microsystems/Oracle Corporation. By downloading the GlassFish Server or the JDK 6, a copy of Java DB is already included in the installation file.

If you feel like learning more about Apache Derby and Java DB, visit the following links:

For Java DB, visit `http://www.oracle.com/technetwork/java/javadb/overview/index.html`.

For downloading JavaDB, visit `http://download.oracle.com/docs/cd/E17413_01/javadb/index.html`.

And for Apache Derby, go to `http://db.apache.org/derby/`.

Getting ready

If your version of NetBeans included GlassFish Server, Java DB is already registered.

However, if this is not the case, and the NetBeans Java SE installation package was chosen, then setup and registration of Java DB needs to be done manually.

Navigate to `http://www.oracle.com/technetwork/java/javadb/downloads/index.html` and download Java DB to the platform of your choice.

How to do it...

To register Java DB with NetBeans:

1. Right-click on **Java DB** node inside the **Databases** subsection of **Services** window.

2. In the Java DB **Properties** window, enter the installation folder of Java DB.

3. **Database Location** is where the Java DB settings will be placed:

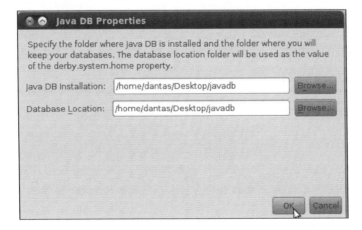

4. Click **OK**.

How it works...

When clicking **OK** under the **Java DB properties** window, the Java DB node will have **Sample** as the child, it is the **Sample** database that already exists in Java DB. A database connection, with Java DB values, is appended to the end of the Databases subsection.

There's more...

Viewing data using the SQL editor.

Viewing data

With Java DB registered and connected, it is possible with a few mouse clicks, to see the data in a Database from within the IDE:

1. Expand the **Sample** connection until **Tables** is shown.

2. Then right-click on a table, for example **CUSTOMER**, and select **View Data...**.

The built-in SQL editor will be shown with the query:

```
select * from APP.CUSTOMER
```

And a grid with the present data is available.

Below is a screenshot of NetBeans with **View Data...** submenu, built-in SQL editor, and data grid:

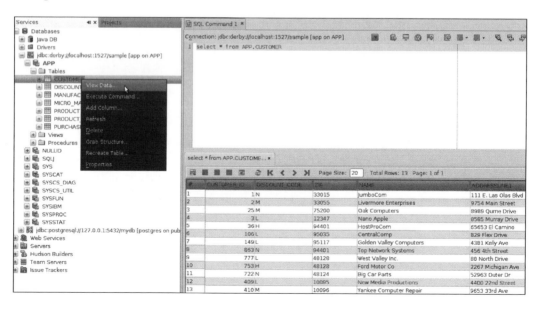

Setting up with Oracle

Now it is time for us to setup the biggest, most important, and best known player in the database world: Oracle.

Oracle's database system is considered by many to be the most feature-complete, functional, and reliable database system on the market. Different versions are suited for different needs and can range from free cut-down versions to full blown suites, with every possible feature and tweak.

Getting ready

There are many versions that can be used with NetBeans. The version we will use for this recipe is the **Oracle 10g Express Edition**. It is free to develop for and fairly easy to install.

It is necessary to have **Oracle 10g Express Edition** installed on the system and fully configured. In this recipe, we will demonstrate only how to make Oracle accessible from within NetBeans.

Here's where to find Oracle 10g Express Edition:

```
http://www.oracle.com/technology/software/products/database/xe/index.html
```

For this recipe to work, it is also necessary to download the JDBC driver, named `ojdbc14.jar`, so it can interface between NetBeans and the Database.

Visit the page below to download the driver:

```
http://www.oracle.com/technology/software/tech/java/sqlj_jdbc/index.html
```

Once the Database is installed and running, and the JDBC driver downloaded, we can proceed to configure NetBeans.

How to do it...

Navigate to the **Services** window:

Adding a new driver:

1. Right-click on **Databases** subsection and select **New Connection...**.

2. When **New Database Connection** window opens, click on the **Driver Name** drop-down and select **New Driver....**

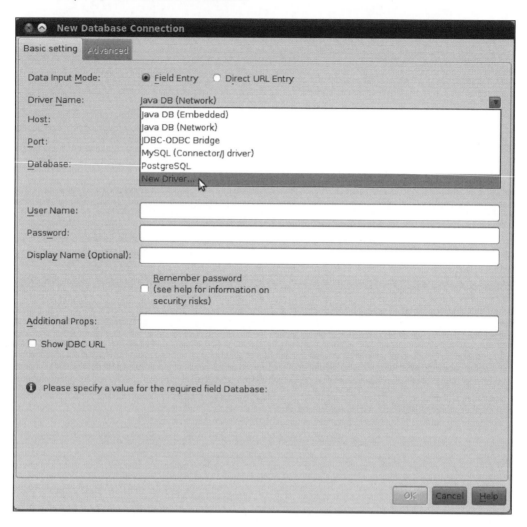

3. When selecting **New Driver...** under the drop-down, the **New JDBC Driver** window will pop-up.

4. Then click on **Add...** and navigate to the location of the driver JAR file.

5. When selecting the driver, the Driver Class will be changed to **oracle.jdbc. OracleDriver** and **Oracle Thin** under **Name**.

6. Click **OK**.

The control then returns to the **New Database Connection** window.

The next step is to enter basic database information.

Note that the following information is not set in stone and you might have changed it when installing and configuring the database. So if all the defaults were used, it is possible that all the information is the same as presented here:

▶ **Host**: localhost
▶ **Port**: 1521
▶ **Service ID**: XE
▶ **User**: system
▶ **password**: the password that was entered during installation
▶ Click on **Show JDBC URL**.

Now that everything looks more or less like the following, it is important to notice the pattern of the JDBC URL:

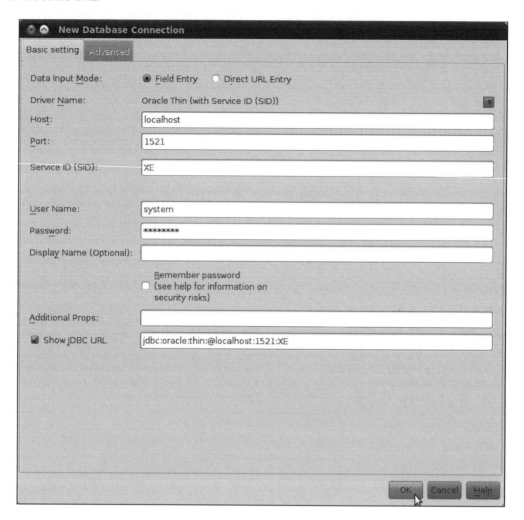

Click **OK** and the control will be passed to the **Advanced** tab, select `system` as the **Schema** (or one of your choice), and click **OK**.

How it works...

This is the first database in this Cookbook that is required to find a JAR file to connect properly.

This is because NetBeans is not providing the JAR file from its package by default. NetBeans provides drivers for MySQL and together with GlassFish Server, also Java DB.

As shown in the registration procedure, after entering the required information, it is important to notice the format of the URL, which needs to be:

```
jdbc:oracle:thin:@localhost:1521:XE
```

XE comes from Express Edition and this is the desired format.

Built-in SQL editor

NetBeans has a great integration with various Databases from various vendors. But it does not stop there; integrated into the IDE is a basic SQL editor. It might not be as powerful as the solutions provided by other vendors, such as PGAdmin or MySQL Query Browser, but it is not intended to replace those tools. Instead, it is a fast way to check data and SQL queries without leaving the comfort of your favorite IDE.

In this recipe, we will see how to use the SQL editor to create databases and tables, how to use the SQL Editor, and also how to use NetBeans integrated UI for managing tables and databases.

Getting ready

Java DB will be used as the primary database for this recipe, but other DB will, of course, work as well. While using Java DB, it is necessary to have it configured and running, if unsure how to perform the required configuration, please refer to the recipe *Setting up with Apache Derby/Java DB* in this chapter.

How to do it...

Let's create a database.

With NetBeans open and Java DB server started:

1. Navigate to the **Services** window and expand the **Databases** node.
2. Right-click on **Java DB** and select **Create Databases...**.
3. The **Create Java DB Database** window will pop up, then enter the following information:
   - ❑ **Database Name**: nbcookbook
   - ❑ **User Name**: test
   - ❑ **Password**: test
   - ❑ **Confirm Password**: test
   - ❑ **Database Location**: Leave the default
4. Press **OK**.

The **Create Java DB Database** window is as follows:

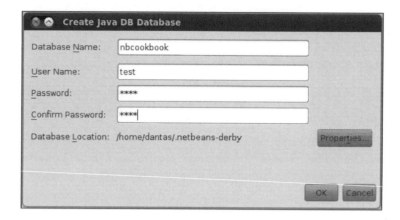

The IDE will execute the required SQL queries for database creation and, upon creation, will place two more icons in the Databases subsection:

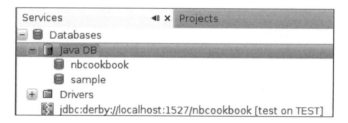

Right-click on **jdbc:derby://localhost:1527/nbcookbook** and select **Connect...**.

After completing the database creation, we will focus on how to create tables:

1. Expand the connection node of **nbcookbook** and then expand the **APP** table.

2. Right-click on Tables under **APP** and select **Create Table...**.

3. Under Table Name, write Address.

4. Click on the **Add Column button**.

5. On the **Add Column** window, enter the following info:

   ❑ **Name**: id

   ❑ **Type**: INTEGER

6. On constraints, click on **Primary key** and **Unique** will be automatically selected.

7. Click **OK** to return to **Create a Table**.

An example of **Add Column** window for the **Primary key** is as follows:

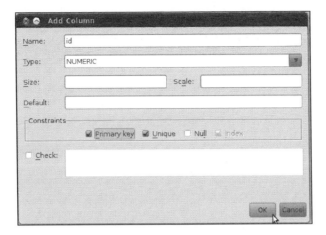

Continue adding columns until the table looks like this:

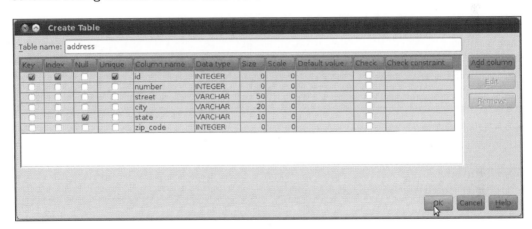

With everything in place, we will insert Data using SQL editor.

1. To execute a command, right-click on the connection and select **Execute Command...**.

2. Inside the SQL Editor, type:

   ```
   insert into app.address values (0, 123, 'Avenue des Champs-
   Élysées', 'Paris', null, 0987)
   ```

3. To execute the command, either click the button as shown below or press *Ctrl+Shift+E* (shortcut).

4. Finally, let's check the contents of our created database.

5. Clean the contents of the SQL Editor and type:

```
select * from app.address
```

6. To execute the command, either click the button shown below or press *Ctrl+Shift+E* (shortcut):

The SQL Editor is then split in two parts; one with the SQL statement and the other with the data from the Address table:

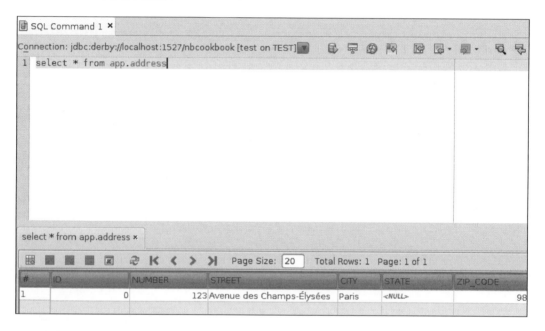

How it works...

There is not much mystery on how the IDE accomplishes the work here. It is very straightforward.

For creating a database and table using the GUI, the IDE simply translates those GUI parameters into SQL queries and through the connection to the database, executes those statements.

Using the **Command Execution** is not much different but instead of using the GUI to build a SQL query, the IDE simply executes the statement provided by the user.

Under Java DB, we have the Databases:

> ▶ **Sample**: It is just some sample database that came by default with the Java DB
>
> ▶ **nbcookbook**: It is our newly created database

Under **Drivers**, a connection to the database can be seen, but by default in the Disconnected mode.

Expanding the nodes of the newly created table, Address, it is possible to see how NetBeans conveniently shows the columns of that particular table:

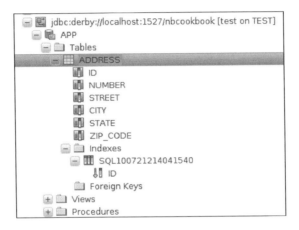

The connection icon changes according to the connection itself. If connected, the icon is the one above; if disconnected, the icon changes to:

There's more...

Working with multiple connections inside the SQL is very easy. Feeling lazy with those inserts? NetBeans to the rescue!

Select connection on editor

In this recipe, we just used one connection to one Database, but it is possible to use multiple connections to different databases and different severs from within the comfort of NetBeans.

Simply select **Connection** on the top of the SQL Editor and the SQL statement inside the editor will be used in that particular database.

For example:

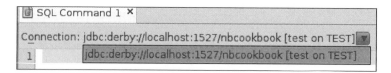

Insert record button

The insert record button is a convenient way to add some rows to the table that is currently being accessed.

Here is the location of the button:

On pressing that button, a new dialog is opened—the **Insert Records** dialog. As the name suggests, it allows the user to insert one or multiple records.

When the dialog box shows up, it's possible to click in the fields and just type the values, as in other database tools.

There is a very nice **Show SQL** button where the user can check the build-up of the insert statement.

For now, we will insert only one row:

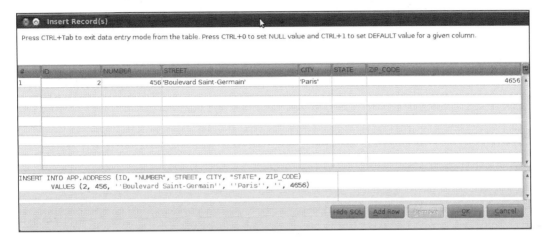

After entering the values as above, press **OK** and the IDE will execute the statement. The new row is added to the Database and, the table is refreshed with the new data. The select statement window from the recipe remains open.

5
Building Web Applications

In this chapter, we will cover:

- ▶ Creating a Web Project using the Wizard
- ▶ Introduction to Java EE 6 using NetBeans
- ▶ Adding JSF as a web Framework
- ▶ Using JSF as a web Framework
- ▶ Using Apache Struts as a web Framework
- ▶ Using GWT as a web Framework

Introduction

Not so long ago, desktop applications prevailed. They ranged from word processors, through e-mail clients, photo editing tools and instant messaging, to games. Internet connections were slow and expensive. Those applications had a very long cycle of development and were, more often than not, very platform-dependent.

With the advance in the Internet speed and the maturing of technologies such as HTML5 and Ajax, applications that reigned supreme on the desktop started to make way for the "cloud".

The applications previously mentioned now live on the Internet. Users tend to see new features added at a much faster pace than before, and are no longer tied to a specific platform or device. The browser has become the window in which Web Applications and media are accessed. By accessing applications through the web browser, deployment is simplified for the end user in comparison to desktop technologies, as updates for web applications are transparent.

Web applications are ubiquitous, and many big companies invest heavily in them, either by selling software and equipment that makes web applications possible, like Oracle and IBM, or by employing different technologies and creating new applications, like Facebook and Google.

Creating a web project using the wizard

As stated in the title of this recipe, we will start with a Web Project.

This Web Project will be the basis for later recipes.

Getting ready

It is required to have NetBeans with Java EE support installed to continue with this and the following recipes.

If this version is not available on your machine, please visit:

```
http://netbeans.org/downloads/index.html
```

There are two **application servers** in this installation package and either Apache Tomcat or GlassFish can be chosen, but at least one is necessary.

An application server is a software framework layer that enables developers to access components by calling APIs defined by the platform in which the Application Server runs. They also provide security, state maintenance, data access, and persistence.

This recipe is demonstrated with Apache Tomcat.

How to do it...

Right-click on the projects window, and select **New Project**:

1. A **New Projects** dialog is shown. Under **Categories**, select **Java Web** and under **Projects**, select **Web Application**, and then click **Next >**.

2. In **Name and Location**:

   ❑ Type `WebApplicationCookbook` under **Project Name**.

   ❑ Leave **Project Location** with the default value.

   ❑ Leave **Project Folder** with the default value.

   ❑ Select **Use Dedicated Folder for Storing Libraries** if not marked.

   ❑ Select **Set as Main Project**.

3. Click **Next >**.

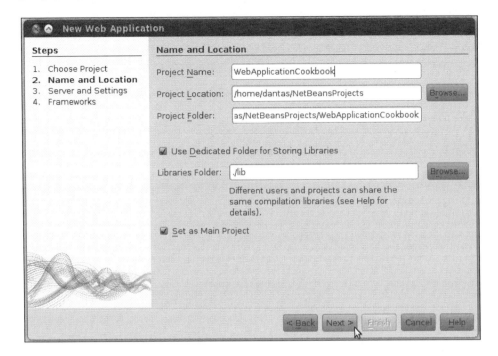

4. In **Server and Settings**, leave all the default values checked:

   ❑ **Server** : Apache Tomcat

   ❑ **Java EE version** : Java EE 6 Web

   ❑ **Context Path:** /WebApplicationCookbook

   And click on Enable Context and Dependency Injection.

5. Click **Next >**.

6. In **Frameworks**, click **Finish**.

To run the project, right-click on **WebApplicationCookbook**, and select **Run**.

The application is compiled, Apache Tomcat is started, and the default system browser opens the index.jsp file.

In NetBeans, the **HTTP Server Monitor** is run alongside the Application.

How it works...

NetBeans creates a complete file structure for our project.

It automatically creates special directories for testing and source classes, writes down configuration files and copies the necessary libraries.

Let's go through what each file and folder means:

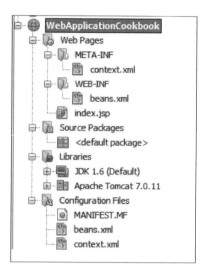

There are two folders under **Web Pages**.

The root folder contains **index.jsp**, the file which is accessed first by our users. The first page that the users will access can be changed in **web.xml**.

- ▶ **META-INF**: This contains **context.xml**, which configures the path in which we will access our application: /WebApplicationCookbook. If defaults were used when setting up Apache Tomcat, then the address used in the browser to access the application will be http://localhost:8080/WebApplicationCookbook.

- ▶ **WEB-INF**: This contains **web.xml**, which configures the way the application behaves and how it should be linked to the application server.

Source Packages and **Test Packages** are empty since we have not created any files yet. The package names give a good idea what they are supposed to hold. Source files hold normal java classes, servlets, POJOs; Test Packages hold files related to JUnit testing classes. The Libraries node contains the **JDK 6** required libraries and the **Apache Tomcat 7.0.11** libraries (or the version which was shipped by default with NetBeans).

The Test Libraries Package contains the JUnit libraries.

The Configuration package contains the following three files:

- ▶ **MANIFEST.MF**: Created and maintained by NetBeans; this file has information about the files packaged inside the WAR.
- ▶ **context.xml**: This is the application server configuration file.
- ▶ **beans.xml**: It is the bean descriptor for the project. This is used by CDI to let Apache Tomcat know that our project contains CDI beans.

There's more...

Peeking at the HTTP Requests.

HTTP Server Monitor

While running the application, NetBeans fires up the **HTTP Server Monitor**. This is used to analyze the information that is exchanged between the browser and the Application Server in real-time.

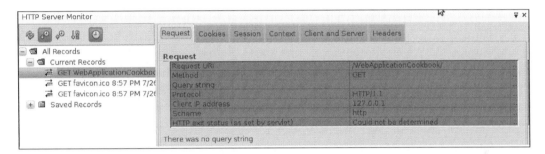

On the left-hand side of the previous screenshot, under **Current Records**, the requests made from the client to the browser are listed. By clicking on each one of those requests shows information related to that particular request is then presented. There are a number of tabs that can be used to monitor different sorts of information:

- ▶ **Request** : Displays the request information.
- ▶ **Cookies** : Displays cookies related to this user.
- ▶ **Session** : Shows the current session information.
- ▶ **Context** : Has information about the servlet context.
- ▶ **Client and Server**: Displays the client data, such as the IP address and the software used to access the application. Same goes for the Server part, which displays information relevant to access configuration, ports, hostname, and so on, of the server.

▶ **Headers** : Displays the HTTP headers contained in the request.

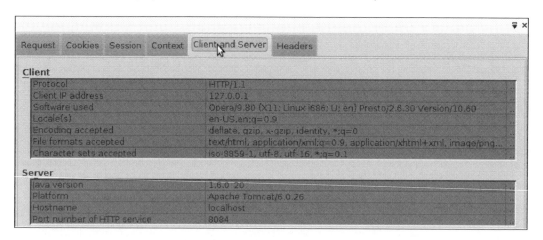

It is also possible to right-click on each individual request and choose **Save**, **Replay**, **Edit and Replay...**, and **Delete**. Selecting **Edit and Replay** will let the user edit the request, change the parameters, request methods, request URL, and so on.

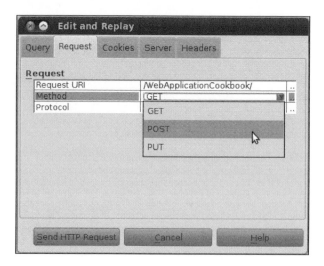

This is a very handy tool when testing and deploying web applications. There are many other, more powerful tools that do the same thing, but they do not offer the simplicity in configuration, and mainly are not free and not that tightly integrated with NetBeans.

Introduction to Java EE 6 using NetBeans

Java EE is a remarkable technology for all that it can accomplish, but it has been plagued by criticism of being overly complicated and verbose.

Much of this criticism was justified for the fact that Java EE relies heavily on XML-based configuration, requiring many interfaces and exceptions, presenting developers with many hurdles to face when using it. Technologies like Hibernate and Spring emerged, and gained much attraction simply because they sought to address those complexities.

With the introduction of Java EE 5, the core platform once again gained the upper hand, trying the same formula that helped catapult Hibernate and Spring into developers' favor. Annotations were brought in, to tone down the verbosity of the code, along with reduction of checked exceptions, POJO programming, introduction of JSF, enhancements in EJB QL and Application Container, and simplification of Session Beans.

Session Beans are Java objects that perform a multitude of operations but are mainly used for storing data. As with Java EE 5, Session Beans can be either Stateless or Stateful.

▶ **Stateful Session Beans** maintain a conversational state for the entire client session.

▶ **Stateless Session Beans** do not maintain a conversational state. These beans are maintained in memory for as long as the client request takes and after that, the state is no longer kept in memory.

The idea of simplifying development continues in Java EE 6. To start, some of the "fat" Java EE acquired during its lifetime is being burned by pruning some outdated technologies. API's such as JAXR, EJB 2.x Entity Beans, Java EE Application Deployment, and others have been marked as "pruned", either for low usage by developers, or for not being entirely implemented by the vendors that chose to create the Application Containers.

On top of that, performance enhancements for deployment and resources used, such as Java EE Web Profiles, were added so that developers that do not utilize the entire Java EE stack can deploy applications based only on what they use.

Updated API's, such as JAX-RS 1.1, EJB 3.1, JPA 2.0, were also introduced in Java EE 6.

If you wish to know more about the technologies in Java EE 6 visit:

▶ Java EE 6: `http://jcp.org/en/jsr/detail?id=316`

▶ EJB 3.1: `http://jcp.org/en/jsr/detail?id=318`

▶ JSF 2.0: `http://jcp.org/en/jsr/detail?id=314`

▶ JSP 2.2: `http://jcp.org/en/jsr/detail?id=245`

▶ Servlet 3.0: `http://jcp.org/en/jsr/detail?id=315`

▶ JPA 2.0: `http://jcp.org/en/jsr/detail?id=317`

NetBeans is the first IDE to have complete support for Java EE 6.

Here are some of the benefits of using NetBeans with Java EE 6:

The editor houses the JSF components, as follows:

▶ Wizards that let the developer create JSF CRUDs. CRUDs is an acronym for Create-Read-Update-Delete, the basic operations for different entities in a web application.

▶ Creation of JSF pages from the Entity Classes.

▶ Entity relationships are supported straight from NetBeans.

▶ Integration with the latest GlassFish Server and more.

Getting ready

Please refer to the recipe *Creating a Web Project using the Wizard* for project creation and the necessary tools to proceed with this recipe.

How to do it...

We will create a New Project based on Java EE 6 Web. The necessary steps are as follows:

1. Right-click on the **Projects** window and select **New Project...** or press *CTRL+SHIFT+N* (shortcut).

2. On **New Project** window: under **Categories**, select **Java Web** and under **Projects**, select **Web Application**, then click **Next**.

3. **Name and Location**: under **Project Name**, write **FirstJavaEE6Application**, and click **Next**.

4. **Server and Settings**:

   ❑ **Server**: GlassFish Server 3.1

   ❑ **Java EE Version**: Java EE 6 Web

   ❑ **Context Path**: leave the default value

5. Click **Next**.

6. In **Frameworks**: click **Finish**.

Upon clicking on the **Finish** button, NetBeans creates a project structure for us.

The created structure is shown in the following screenshot:

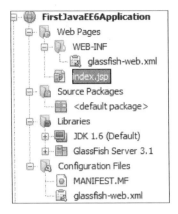

The new project is created under the Projects window and a default JSP file is opened in the editor under the name `index.jsp`.

We will then proceed by adding a Servlet.

1. Right-click on **FirstJavaEE6Application** and select **New**, and then click on **Servlet...**.

2. Under **Name and Location**: under **Class Name**, write **FirstServlet**, leave **Location** pointing to **Source Packages** and under **Package**, write **servlets** and click **Finish**.

A new Servlet is added to the project structure and the `FirstServlet.java` file is opened in the editor.

Our next step is to add an Enterprise JavaBean (EJB):

1. Right-click on **FirstJavaEE6Application** and select **New**; then click on **Session Bean...** or *Ctrl+N* (shortcut).

2. Under **Categories**, select **Java EE** and under **File Types**, select **Session Bean**, then click **Next**.

3. **Name and Location**:
   - ❑ under **EJB Name**, write **FirstEJB**
   - ❑ leave **Project and Location** with default values
   - ❑ under **Package**, type **ejbs**
   - ❑ **Session Type** should be marked with **Stateless** and leave **Create Interface** unmarked

4. Click **Finish**.

This will generate the EJB POJO and the `FirstEJB.java` will be shown in the editor.

With `FirstEJB.java` open, let's add some behavior to it:

1. Right-click inside the body of the class and select **Insert Code...** or press *Alt+Insert* (shortcut).
2. Select **Add Business Method...**.
3. Under **Name**, type: `reverseString`.
4. In **Return type**, write `String`.
5. Then click on **Add** and under **name**, type `normalString`.
6. Click **OK**.

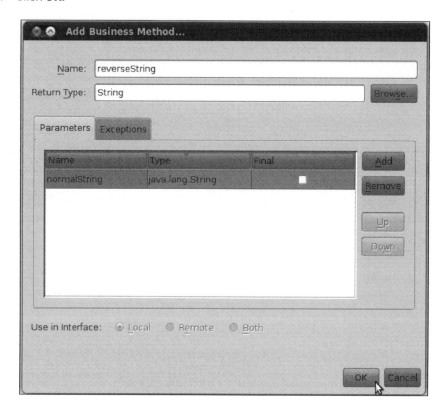

Inside the `reverseString` method, type:

```
return new StringBuffer(normalString).reverse().toString();
```

The whole class will look like this:

```
package ejbs;

import javax.ejb.Stateless;

@Stateless
public class FirstEJB {
    public String reverseString(String normalString) {
        return new StringBuffer(normalString).reverse().toString();
    }
}
```

We need to call the EJB from within the Servlet. So inside of `FirstServlet.java`, type:

```
@EJB FirstEJB firstEJB;
```

And resolve the import by leaving the cursor on top of the FirstEJB declaration and press _Alt+Enter_.

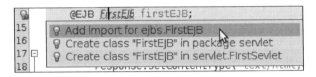

Click **Add import for ejbs.FirstEJB** and the import error is resolved.

Then replace the code inside the try-catch block, the one that is commented out, with:

```
            out.println("<html>");
            out.println("<body>");
            out.println("<h1>FirstSevlet backwards is "+ firstEJB.
    reverseString("FirstServlet") +"</h1>");
            out.println("</body>");
            out.println("</html>");
```

Click on the **Save** button.

With all the codes in place, all that is left for us is to run our project.

1. After saving the `FirstServlet.java`, right-click on **FirstJavaEE6Application** and select **Run**.

2. When the browser opens showing the contents of `index.jsp`, replace the URL with `http://localhost:8080/FirstJavaEE6Application/FirstServlet`

The contents of the web page will then turn to:

FirstServlet backwards is telvreStsriF

How it works...

When the user clicks the **Finish** button in the **Project Creation** step, NetBeans creates the project structure and the configuration files necessary for this project to run in the Application Server.

Note that when adding a Servlet, the IDE generates the `doGet` and `doPost` methods and adds a method call to the `processRequest` method. While this is a nice way of forcing all traffic from a servlet to be tunneled in one method, in the real world you might want to change that by being more specific in what is needed from your `doGet()` or `doPost()` methods.

Note that an `index.jsp` file is created and opened, by default, in the code editor.

Our first Session Bean, called FirstEJB, is a Stateless session bean. This means that the Session Bean will not maintain a conversational state for a specific client. When the request is processed by the bean and execution is returned to the servlet, the bean will not hold store any information about the request.

After removing all the comments from FirstEJB, it is noticeable how small that EJB looks.

The `reverseString()` business method that we have created for our Session Bean returns a reverse string to the client. This method call is used from the Servlet. The Servlet can access the Session Bean, thanks to the Dependency Injection we are performing.

The Dependency Injection code, or simply DI, is:

```
@EJB FirstEJB firstEJB;
```

DI is a mechanism employed by Application Servers to instantiate and assign a certain object to the reference used. In our case, GlassFish sees the `@EJB` annotation before the FirstEJB class name and assigns a new Object of that type to the FirstEJB reference.

The call to the PrintWriter will then output the information as an HTML page, a rather cumbersome way of writing HTML, but enough for our example, and also output the reverseString method call and place the output in the middle of our HTML code.

Java EE 6 Web Profile is a smaller subset of the entire Java EE stack. As mentioned previously, this is very useful when not all API's are needed for a certain project, making it lighter to run and less resource-hungry. This not only makes better use of the resources we have but also makes life less complicated when maintaining a certain application.

There's more...

Let's write some JUnit tests to our EJB's and check the changes that Java EE 6 and GlassFish deploy on Save.

Writing JUnit tests to your EJB

1. Right-click on `FirstEJB.java`, select **Tools**, and then click on **Create JUnit Tests**.

2. The **Select JUnit Version** dialog will pop-up, select **JUnit 4.x**, and click **Select**.

3. The **Create Tests** dialog is presented; de-select **JavaDoc Comments** and **Source Code Hints** under **Generated Comments**.

4. Click **OK**.

Replace the contents of `testReverseString` with:

```
System.out.println("reverseString");
String normalString = "raw";
FirstEJB instance = (FirstEJB)javax.ejb.embeddable.
EJBContainer.createEJBContainer().getContext().
lookup("java:global/classes/FirstEJB");
String expResult = "war";
String result = instance.reverseString(normalString);
assertEquals(expResult, result);
```

Press *Shift+F6* to run the JUnit.

The **Test Results** window will appear with the list of **Passed Tests** and the **Output** of GlassFish Server.

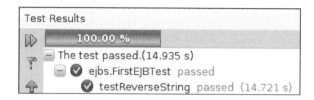

The Embeddable EJB Container is a new API in Java EE 6 and can be checked by visiting:

`http://jcp.org/aboutJava/communityprocess/final/jsr318/index.html`

This API further simplifies the way JUnit tests can be written to test EJBs.

Deployment descriptor is optional when creating servlets

This is yet another new feature in Java EE 6 present in the Servlet 3.0 specification.

The entire configuration which was previously stored in XML is now transferred and implemented with annotations within the Servlet itself.

An example of annotation in our Servlet is:

```
@WebServlet(name="FirstServlet", urlPatterns={"/FirstServlet"})
```

Notice that we have not touched any configuration files. If you are new to Java EE world, this will not sound so groundbreaking, but for those with more experience in the field, this is a very good addition to the platform.

Deploy on Save

It is well-known that NetBeans offers a handy integration with GlassFish Server.

One of these features is Deploy on Save. Every time a file, JSP, or servlet for example, is saved on the editor, NetBeans notifies the container and deploys the file for usage.

Although handy, not everyone might want or enjoy this feature. This is mainly because application dependencies might be broken when changes are deployed.

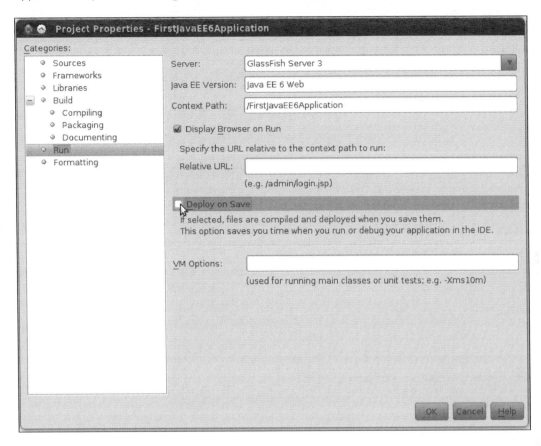

To turn this feature off:

1. Right-click on the **Projects** name, `FirstJavaEE6Application`, and select **Properties**.

2. Under **Categories**, click on **Run** and de-select **Deploy** in the **Save** option.

3. Click **OK**.

Note that this will force manual deployment.

Adding JSF as a web framework

JSP was great in its time. It revolutionized the way developers generated dynamic content on the web. But as with everything, time passed and other technologies were developed that made it even easier to generate this same kind of content, and on top of that, overcame many of the limitations that were introduced with JSP.

Enter JSF. It brings a graphical development mentality, similar to Swing's, which relies on a set of reusable UI components and event-driven approach. Instead of totally breaking away from its roots, JSF 2.0 can also be developed in the same way JSP is; in fact, a JSF application is a JSP/servlets application. Typically, Web Applications are developed using the MVC design pattern. This pattern works great with JSF since, in a typical JSF application, the View is the page we write, the Model is the data we wish to show, and the Controller is the FacesServlet. Every request passes through the FacesServlet. The configuration file for the FacesServlet is `faces-config.xml`.

If you wish to learn more about JSF, visit:

`http://www.jcp.org/en/jsr/detail?id=314`

`http://www.oracle.com/technetwork/java/javaee/download-139288.html`

`http://www.oracle.com/technetwork/java/javaee/javaserverfaces-139869.html`

Getting ready

We will use the sources of the previously created Java EE 6 project. If unsure how to do this, refer to *Introduction to Java EE 6 using NetBeans* in the *Creating a new Project* sub-section available in this chapter.

It is also possible to use available sources from your own Java web project.

Java DB must be installed and configured. It is necessary to have a connection to the sample database. Refer to Chapter 04, *JDBC and NetBeans*, to learn how to do it if unsure.

How to do it...

Navigate to the **Projects** window:

1. Right-click on the projects name, in our case `FirstJavaEE6Application`, and select **Properties**.

2. On the **Project Properties** dialog, select **Frameworks**, and on **Used Frameworks**, click on **Add...**.

3. Under **Add a Framework** dialog, select **JavaServer Faces**, and click **OK**.

4. Leave all the default values under **Libraries and Configuration** unchanged.

5. Click **OK**.

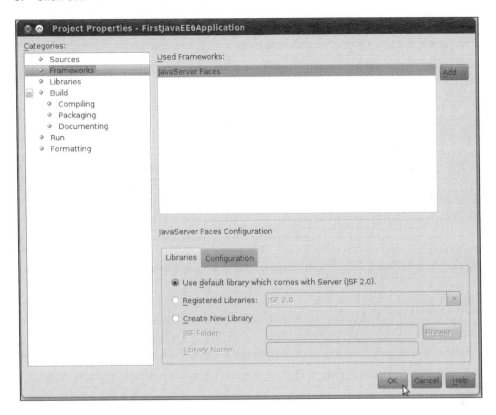

How it works...

After adding JavaServer Faces, NetBeans creates an `index.xhtml` under the **Web Pages** folder.

`index.xhtml` is our entry point of JSF for the time being.

There's more...

Here is how to run `index.xhtml` on your browser.

Running index.xhtml

To execute `index.xhtml`:

Right-click on `index.xhtml` and select **Run File** or use the *Shift+F6* shortcut when the page is open in the editor.

The output will have GlassFish's start-up logs, and the default system browser will show a **Hello** from the Facelets page.

Using JSF as a web framework

In this recipe, we will put into practice some of the goodies that JSF packs, and that NetBeans makes it easier for the developer to take advantage of.

In this recipe, we will create a JSF CRUD. To access the CRUD, the user is forced to pass through the login page, which we will develop using Managed Beans. On the top of all that, we will add templates to each and every page created, giving a more consistent look across the application.

Getting ready

It is also possible to use available sources from your own Java Web project. Java DB must be installed and configured. It is necessary to have a connection to the sample database. Refer to Chapter 04, *JDBC and NetBeans*, to learn how to do it if unsure.

How to do it...

We need to add a Login page with the success and failure flow.

1. Right-click on `FirstJavaEE6Application` and select **New and JSF Page...**.
2. Execute the following steps in the **New JSF Page** dialog:
   - ❏ **Name and Location**: Under **Files Name**, type `login`
   - ❏ Under **Folder** text field, type **pages**
   - ❏ The **selected Options** must be **Facelets**
3. And click **Finish**.

When the `login.xhtml` opens in the Editor, replace:

```
<h:head>
  <title>Facelet Title</title>
</h:head>
<h:body>
  Hello from Facelets
</h:body>
```

with:

```
<h:head>
    <title>Login</title>
  <h:outputStylesheet name="css/jsfcrud.css"/>
</h:head>
<h:body>
    <ui:composition template="/template.xhtml">
        <ui:define name="body">
            <h:form>
                <h:panelGrid rowClasses="3" >
                    <h:outputText value
                                  ="user name: " />
                    <h:inputText id=
                                 "loginname" value="#{Validator.
username}" />
                    <h:outputText value=
                                  "password: " />
                    <h:inputSecret id=
                                   "password" value="#{Validator.
password}" />
                    <h:commandButton value=
                                     "submit" action="#{Validator.
VerifyUsernameAndPassword}" />
                </h:panelGrid>
            </h:form>
        </ui:define>
    </ui:composition>
</h:body>
```

The editor will show some import errors, so let's click on the bulb icon and fix them:

Let's repeat the same process for the failure page:

1. Right-click on `FirstJavaEE6Application` and select **New** and **JSF Page...**.

2. Execute the following steps in the **New JSF Page** dialog:

    ❑ **Name and Location**: Under **Files Name**, type `failure`

    ❑ Under **Folder** text field, type `pages`

3. The selected **Options** must be **Facelets**.

4. Click **Finish**.

When the `failure.xhtml` opens in the Editor, replace:

```
<h:head>
  <title>Facelet Title</title>
</h:head>
<h:body>
  Hello from Facelets
</h:body>
```

with:

```
<h:head>
    <title>Error</title>
</h:head>
<h:body>
    <ui:composition template="/template.xhtml">
        <ui:define name="body">
            username/password incorrect.
        </ui:define>
    </ui:composition>
</h:body>
```

Resolve the import problems again as above then save all the files.

Our next step is to create **entities** from our database. Check the following steps:

1. Right-click on `FirstJavaEE6Application` and select **New** and **Entity Classes from Database....**

2. Under **Database Tables**: With the **New Entity Classes from Database** dialog open:

    ❑   Click on the drop-down in **Data Source** and select `jdbc/sample`.

    ❑   When the **Available Tables** finish being populated, select **PRODUCT** and click **Add**.

3. Click **Next**.

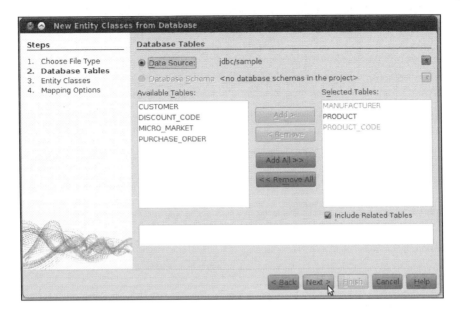

4. Under **Entity Classes**: Leave **Class Names**, **Project**, **Location**, **Generated Named Query Annotations for Persistence Fields**, and **Create Persistence Unit** with the default values.

5. Under **Package**, type `entities`.

6. Click **Finish**.

Package and contents created by following the above steps is shown below:

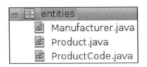

After importing entities from the database, we will create the JSF CRUD from those newly imported Entities:

1. Right-click on `FirstJavaEE6Application` and select **New** and click on **JSF Pages** from **Entity Classes....**

2. **Entity Classes**: Select all of the entity classes; this can be done by pressing *Ctrl+A*, and clicking **Add >**.

3. Leave the **Include Referenced Classes** box ticked.

4. Click **Next >**.

5. **Generate JSF Pages and Classes**: Under **JSF Pages** folder, type **pages** and leave all the other fields with their default values.

6. Click **Finish**.

You can see the following screenshot:

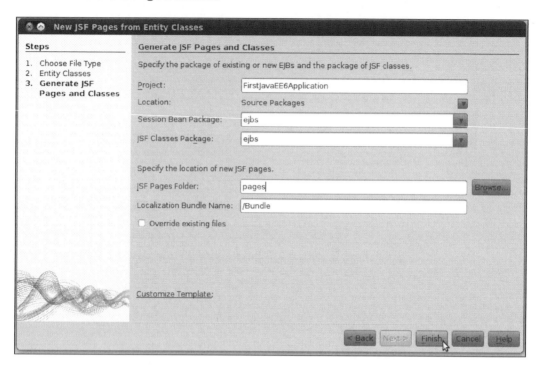

Open the `template.xhtml` and replace the code between to change the facelets template:

```
<h:head>
```

And:

```
</h:body>
```

Tags with:

```
<h:head>
    <meta http-equiv="Content-Type" content="text/html;
charset=UTF-8" />
    <link href="./../../resources/css/default.css"
rel="stylesheet" type="text/css" />
    <link href="./../../resources/css/cssLayout.css"
rel="stylesheet" type="text/css" />
```

```
        <title>Facelets Template</title>
        <h:outputStylesheet name="css/jsfcrud.css"/>
    </h:head>

    <h:body>
        <div id="top" align="center">
            <ui:insert name="top"><h1>The Killer App</h1></ui:insert>
        </div>
        <div id="content" class="center_content">
            <ui:insert name="body">Content</ui:insert>
        </div>
        <div id="bottom" align="right">
            <ui:insert name="bottom"><i><br/>NetBeans Cookbook</i></
ui:insert>
        </div>
    </h:body>
```

Save the file.

Now let's tie those pages together by adding a managed bean and navigation rules.

Navigate to **WEB-INF** and expand the node, then open `faces-config.xml` in the Editor and replace the code before the `<application>` tag with the following:

```
    <managed-bean>
      <managed-bean-name>Validator</managed-bean-name>
      <managed-bean-class>util.Validator</managed-bean-class>
      <managed-bean-scope>request</managed-bean-scope>
    </managed-bean>
    <navigation-rule>
      <from-view-id>/pages/login.xhtml</from-view-id>
      <navigation-case>
        <from-action>#{Validator.VerifyUsernameAndPassword}</from-
action>
        <from-outcome>success</from-outcome>
        <to-view-id>index.xhtml</to-view-id>
      </navigation-case>
      <navigation-case>
        <from-action>#{Validator.VerifyUsernameAndPassword}</from-
action>
        <from-outcome>failure</from-outcome>
        <to-view-id>/pages/failure.xhtml</to-view-id>
      </navigation-case>
    </navigation-rule>
```

Save the file.

The next step is to create the managed bean:

1. Right-click on `FirstJavaEE6Application` and select **New** and **Java Class...**.
2. Under **Name and Location**: under **Class Name**, type `Validator`.
3. Under **Package**, type `util`.
4. Click **Finish**.

Now insert the following code snippet inside the Validator class:

```
String password;
String username;

public String getUsername(){
  return username;
}

public void setUsername(String username){
  this.username = username;
}

public String getPassword(){
  return password;
}

public void setPassword(String password){
  this.password = password;
}

public String VerifyUsernameAndPassword(){
  if(username.equals("admin") && password.equals("admin"))
    return "success";
  else
    return "failure";
}
```

A few things left to do:

Open `index.xhtml` and after the:

```
<h:body>
```

Add:

```
<ui:composition template="/template.xhtml">
  <ui:define name="body">
```

And before:

```
</h:body>
```

Add:

```
</ui:define>
</ui:composition>
```

Once we resolve the import errors, we are ready to deploy the application.

Right-click on **FirstJavaEE6Application** and select **Deploy**.

How it works...

The application can be accessed by deploying it from the IDE and pointing your browser in the direction of:

```
http://localhost:8080/FirstJavaEE6Application/faces/pages/login.xhtml
```

We started with the basics, creating a normal login-success-fail case which is very common in web applications. Even though we did not check the password and user name validity from a database, which is the best case scenario, it would not take much more programming to achieve that goal.

For the facelets template, we created a directory under WEB-INF because we do not wish to make the templates page visible to the world. By creating a directory under WEB-INF, we ensure that nothing under that directory can be accessed externally.

The facelets template ensures that this template is applied to all the pages, to share the same common look. It also makes it easier to add different behavior if necessary.

There's more...

Here is how to use NetBeans to conveniently create your own template.

Creating your own template

Under the Projects window, expand the **FirstJavaEE6Application** node, and then the **Web Pages** node:

1. Right-click on **WEB-INF** and select **New** and then **Folder...**.
2. In the **New Folder** dialog, type **Name and Location**; under **Folder Name**, type `templates`.
3. Click on **Finish**.

To create the Facelets Template:

1. Right-click on the newly-created templates folder and select **Facelets Template...**.

2. In the **New Facelets Template Dialog, Name and Location**: Under **File Name**, type `internal-template`. Leave the other settings with their default values.

3. Under **Layout Style**, select **CSS** and the following design:

4. Click on **Finish**.

The New Facelets Template Dialog should look like the following screenshot:

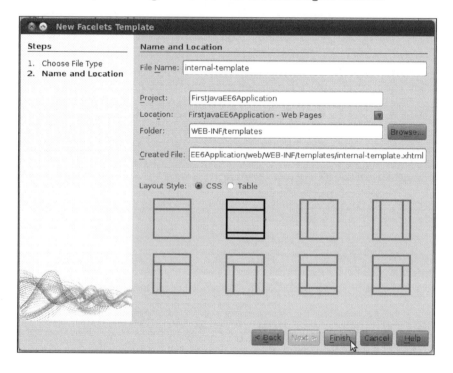

Now you can choose to apply the new Template to your pages.

Using Apache Struts as a web framework

Apache Struts is one of the best-known web frameworks. It is on top of the Java Platform and hosted by the Apache Foundation. Struts is available for free, under the Apache License.

The main goal of Apache Struts is to build web applications with a clear separation between the Model, View, and Controller. As with JSF, there is one focal point of configuration, the `struts-config.xml` and the controller, called ActionServlet, which controls the navigation flow. Other parts of the Struts framework are:

▶ **Action**: Basically these are the requests from the client. The ActionServlet checks the URI to determine which action to call. Actions are used to access the business classes.

▶ **ActionForm**: Beans used by the action to temporarily store and validate data from the form pages.

Struts is one of the many web frameworks supported by NetBeans. The editor makes it possible to add XML configuration tags to `struts-config.xml`, handle ActionServlet and ActionForm, and other features which we will check soon.

How to do it...

We will need to create a New Project and add the Struts Framework along the way. Here's how.

Right-click on the **Projects** window, select **New Project**:

1. A **New Projects** dialog is shown. Under **Categories**, select **Java Web** and under **Projects**, select **Web Application**, and then click **Next**.

2. Under **Name and Location**:
   - ❏ Type **StrutsWebApp** under **Project Name**.
   - ❏ Leave **Project Location** with the default value.
   - ❏ Leave **Project Folder** with the default value.
   - ❏ Select **Use Dedicated Folder for Storing Libraries** if not marked.
   - ❏ Select **Set as Main Project**.

3. Click **Next**.

4. Under **Server and Setting**, enter:
   - ❏ **Server** : Apache Tomcat 7.0.11
   - ❏ **Java EE version** : Java EE 5
   - ❏ **Context Path** : /StrutsWebApp

5. Click **Next**.

6. **Frameworks**: Under the **Frameworks** selection, click on **Struts 1.3.8** (please note that a newer version of Struts might be available from NetBeans IDE; this recipe may work on this version too).

7. Leave all the values in **Action Servlet Name**, **Action URL Pattern**, and **Application Resource** with their default values.

8. Click **Finish**.

IDE adds libraries, configuration files, and opens the welcomeStrutsPage.jsp in the Editor.

The steps for creating the user registration page are as follows:

1. Right-click on **StrutsWebApp**.

2. Select **New** and **JSP....**.

3. When the **New JSP File** dialog opens, under **File Name**, type register-user-page.

4. Leave **Project and Location** with their default values.

5. Under **Folder**, type **pages.**

6. Leave **Options** with **JSP File (Standard Syntax)**.

7. Click **Finish**.

With register-user-page.jsp open in the editor, add the HTML and bean taglibs right after the @page:

```
<%@taglib uri="http://struts.apache.org/tags-html" prefix="html" %>
<%@taglib uri="http://struts.apache.org/tags-bean" prefix="bean" %>
```

And replace the following tag:

```
<h1>Hello World!</h1>
```

With:

```
<html:form action="/register">
    <table border="0">
        <thead>
            <tr>
                <th>Username:</th>
                <th><html:text property="username" /></th>
            </tr>
        </thead>
        <tbody>
            <tr>
```

```
                            <td>Password:</td>
                            <td><html:password property="password"  />
                            </td>
                        </tr>
                        <tr>
                            <td>E-mail</td>
                            <td><html:text property="email" /></td>
                        </tr>
                        <tr>
                            <td>Country:</td>
                            <td>
                                <html:select property="country">
                                    <html:option value="brazil">Brazil</
html:option>

                                    <html:option value="finland">Finland</
html:option>

                                    <html:option value="india">India</
html:option>

                                    <html:option value="usa">USA</
html:option>

                                </html:select>
                            </td>
                        </tr>
                    </tbody>
                </table>
                <html:submit value="Register" />
            </html:form>
```

Next step is to create the success page:

1. Right-click on **StrutsWebApp**.

2. Select **New** and **JSP...**.

3. When the **New JSP File** dialog opens, under **File Name**, type success.

4. Leave **Project and Location** with their default values.

5. Under **Folder**, type **pages**.

6. Leave **Options** with **JSP File (Standard Syntax)**.

7. Click **Finish**.

With success.jsp open in the editor, add the bean taglib to the page right after the @page:

```
<%@taglib uri="http://struts.apache.org/tags-bean" prefix="bean" %>
```

And replace the following tag:

```
<h1>Hello World!</h1>
```

With:

```
User <bean:write name="RegisterForm" property="username" />
successfully created.
```

Since it is a Struts project, we will need to add an ActionForm to our project that will be named as **RegisterForm**.

1. Right-click on **StrutsWebApp**.
2. Select **New** and **Other**.
3. When the **New File** dialog opens; **Choose File Type**: Under **Categories**, select **Struts**.
4. Under **File Types**, select **Struts ActionForm Bean**.
5. Click **Next**.

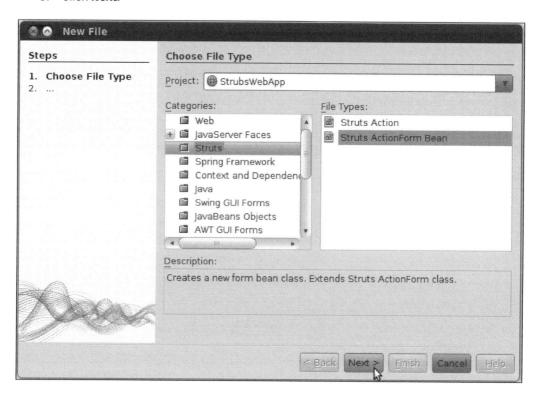

6. Under **Name and Location**:

   ❑ Under **Class Name**, type `RegisterForm`.

   ❑ Leave **Project and Location** with their default values.

   ❑ Under **Package**, type `actionforms`.

   ❑ Leave **Created File**, **Superclass**, and **Configuration File** with their default values.

7. Click **Finish**.

8. Delete the contents of the class and add:

   ```
   private String username;
   private String password;
   private String email;
   private String country;
   ```

9. Then press *Alt+Insert* and when the **Generate** dialog shows up, select **Getter and Setter...**, as shown in the following screenshot:

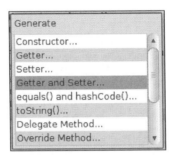

10. Click on all the fields under **Generate Getters and Setters** dialog and click **Generate**.

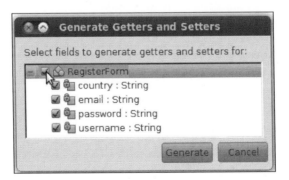

Finally, we will tie everything together by creating the Struts Action.

1. Right-click on **StrutsWebApp**.

2. Select **New** and **Other**.

3. When the **New File** dialog opens, for **Choose File Type**: Under **Categories**, select **Struts**.

4. Under **File Types**, select **Struts Action**.

5. Click **Next >**.

6. **Name** and **Location**:

   ❑ Under **Class Name**, enter `RegisterAction`

   ❑ Leave **Package** and **Source Packages** with their default values

   ❑ Under **Package**, type **actions**

   ❑ Leave **Created File**, **Superclass**, and **Configuration File** with their default values

   ❑ Under **Action Path**, enter `/register`

7. Click **Next**.

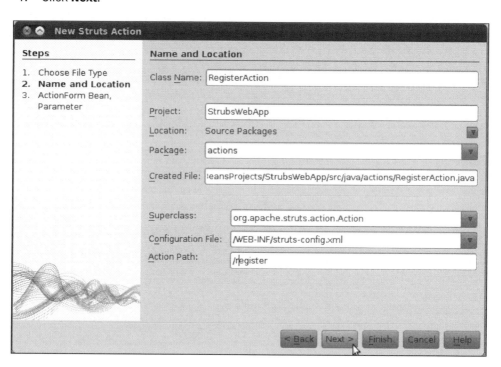

8. **ActionForm Bean, Parameter**:

    ❑   Under **ActionForm Bean Name**, the IDE automatically finds **RegisterForm**

    ❑   On **Input Source**, erase the values from the field

    ❑   For **Scope**, select **Request**

    ❑   Uncheck **Validate ActionForm Bean**

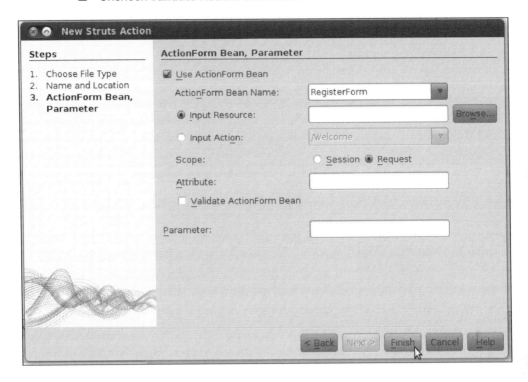

The last detail to add is a forward tag in `struts-config.xml`.

Open `struts-config.xml`:

1. Right-click inside the editor and select **Struts** and **Add Forward**.

2. On the **Add Forward** dialog, enter the following configuration:

    ❑   Under **Forward Name**, type `success`.

    ❑   On the **Forward Top** section, click on **Browse...**.

    ❑   The **Browse Files** dialog opens, expand **Web Pages**, **Pages** and click on `success.jsp`, and click on **Select File**.

    ❑   Back on the **Add Forward** dialog, under the **Location** section, click on **Action**, and select `/register`.

3. Click **Add**.

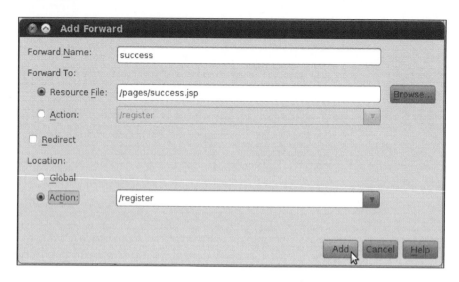

Back on the Project window, navigate to the `register-user-page.jsp`, right-click on it, and select **Run**.

How it works...

In this recipe, we have created a simple case of registering a user.

No database is involved, just a simple way to show how NetBeans handles the very basics of Struts.

In the user registration page, we have the first usage of Struts components in the web page. The components in this page come from the HTML taglib.

`<html:form action="/register">` defines which action is being pointed at after the `<html:submit>` is used.

A combination of `<html:text>`, `<html:password>`, `<html:select>`, and `<html:submit>` are used. The names, by themselves, are very descriptive:

- ▶ `<html:text>` provides a text box
- ▶ `<html:password>` also provides a text box, but with character obfuscation
- ▶ `<html:select>` shows a normal drop box with some countries pre-configured
- ▶ `<html:submit>` triggers the page to be submitted to the corresponding action

We proceed to create our success page. This page confirms that everything went well with the registration of our user, and prints the user name on the screen.

For this to happen, we need to use the bean taglib. This tag requires the ActionForm and the property to be printed:

```
<bean:write name="RegisterForm" property="username" />
```

Readers would have to create their own implementation of Struts ActionForm class/interface. This implementation should contain a few simple String-based properties. NetBeans can help with this by automatically generating getters and setters.

The set is complete by using the IDE to create the action class. The IDE generates the class, adds a temporary implementation of the execute method and inserts an action tag to the `sturts-config.xml`.

Finally, with the IDE's help, we edit `struts-config.xml` once more to add the forward tag with a neat GUI interface.

Using GWT as a web framework

Google Web Toolkit is an open-source development toolkit with Java APIs that help developers easily build dynamic web pages. Development takes place in Java, but the output is JavaScript/AJAX code, abstracting all the quirks that are related to JavaScript development.

The toolkit also provides a widget library that can be extended according to the needs of each developer and each project.

With a third-party plugin called GWT4NB, it is possible to integrate GWT with NetBeans to have all of the facilities from within the IDE, just like a normal NetBeans project.

Currently GWT4NB is only available to the previous version of NetBeans, version 6.8, so if you wish to use the plugin please download NetBeans 6.9 and proceed with the recipe.

If you wish to learn more about GWT visit:

```
http://code.google.com/webtoolkit/doc/latest/DevGuide.html
```

Getting ready

Please refer to the recipe *Creating a Web Project using the Wizard* for project creation and the necessary tools required to proceed with this recipe.

For the Google Web Toolkit visit:

```
http://code.google.com/webtoolkit
```

Download and unpack the SDK to the directory of your choice.

To download GWT4NB, open NetBeans:

1. On the toolbar, click on **Tools** and **Plugins**.

2. In the **Plugins** window, click on **Available Plugins** tab.

3. Search for **GWT4NB** and tick on the box.

4. Click **Install**.

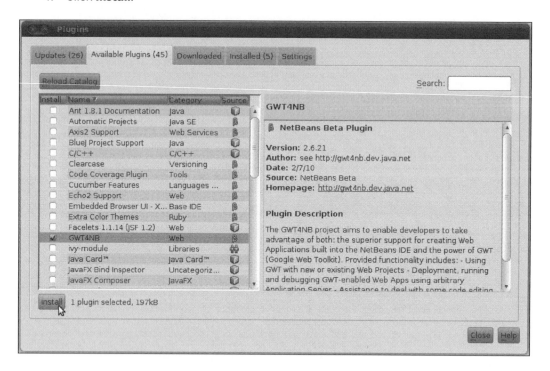

Follow the installation steps on the **NetBeans Plugin Installer Window** until completion.

Notice that all of these tools are necessary for us to continue with our recipe.

With them installed, let's start our recipe.

How to do it...

We will start by creating the GWT Web App project:

1. Right-click on the **Projects** window and select **New Project**.

2. A **New Projects** dialog is shown. Under **Categories**, select **Java Web** and under **Projects**, select **Web Application**, then click **Next >**.

3. For **Name and Location**, type **GWTWebApp** under **Project Name**:

   ❑ Leave **Project Location** with the default value.

   ❑ Leave **Project Folder** with the default value.

   ❑ Select **Use Dedicated Folder for Storing Libraries** if not marked.

   ❑ Select **Set as Main Project**.

4. Click **Next >**.

5. **Server and Setting**, enter:

   ❑ **Server**: GlassFish Server 3

   ❑ **Java EE version**: Java EE 6 Web

   ❑ **Context Path**: /GWTWebApp

6. Click **Next >**.

7. **Frameworks**: Under the **Frameworks** selection, mark **Google Web Toolkit**.

8. The **Google Web Toolkit Configuration** section appears.

9. Click on the **Browse** button under **GWT Installation Folder** to select the folder which GWT has been extracted to.

10. Under **GWT Module**, type com.mybook.Main.

11. Click **Finish**.

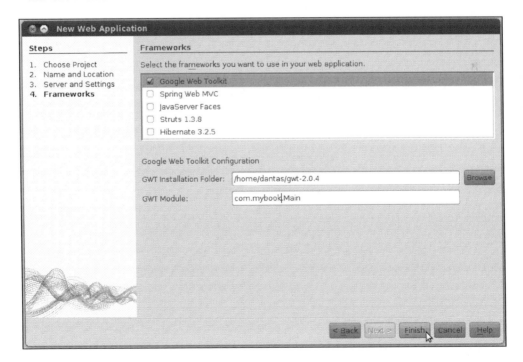

Upon project creation, the IDE will automatically open `Main.gwt.xml`.

Click on its tab and select **XML**:

You can either add or uncomment the line which contains:

```
<inherits name='com.google.gwt.user.theme.standard.Standard'/>
```

To edit `MainEntryPoint.java`, we will need to perform multiple steps, starting by adding local variables.

Right after the class declaration, `public class MainEntryPoint extends EntryPoint`, add:

```java
private final String NETBEANS_LOGO =
"http://netbeans.org/images_www/v5/nb-logo2.gif";
private final String HAPPY_FACE =
"http://upload.wikimedia.org/wikipedia/commons/2/23/Alejoy.gif";
private final String ANGRY_FACE =
"http://upload.wikimedia.org/wikipedia/commons/8/87/
Face-angry_red.png";
private VerticalPanel eastPanel = new VerticalPanel();
private VerticalPanel mainPanel = new VerticalPanel();
private Image netbeansImage = new Image(NETBEANS_LOGO);
private DockLayoutPanel dockLayoutPanel = new
DockLayoutPanel(Unit.EM);
private Tree tree = new Tree();
private TreeItem treeItem = new TreeItem("Social Network");
private DatePicker calendar = new DatePicker();
private final Label eventsLabel = new Label();
private MenuBar outerMenuBar = new MenuBar();
private MenuBar innerItem;
private final TextBox textBox = new TextBox();
private Button shareButton = new Button("Share");
```

Let's resolve the import errors:

Press *Ctrl+Shift+I*.

The **Fix All Imports** window should be exactly like the following screenshot:

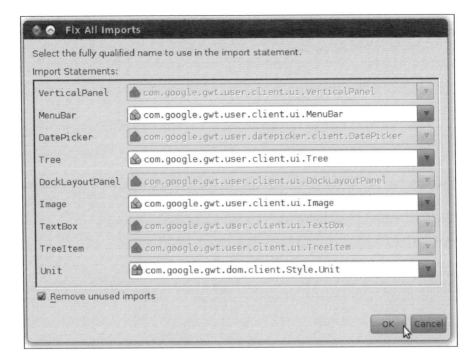

Click **OK** and save the File.

In the same class, let's add the `createTreeItem` method. Right after the `onModuleLoad` method, write the following:

```
private void createTreeItem() {
    treeItem.addItem("Updates");
    treeItem.addItem("Photos");
    treeItem.addItem("Videos");
    treeItem.addItem("Notes").addItem("My note");
    treeItem.addItem(new TreeItem(new CheckBox("Privacy?")));
    tree.setPixelSize(20, 20);
    tree.addItem(treeItem);
}
```

Resolve the import errors by pressing *Ctrl+Shift+I* and save the File.

After the `createTreeItem` method, add:

```
private void createCalendar() {
    calendar.addValueChangeHandler(new ValueChangeHandler() {

        public void onValueChange(ValueChangeEvent event) {
```

```
                Date date = (Date) event.getValue();
                String dateString =
                DateTimeFormat.getMediumDateFormat().format(date);
                eventsLabel.setText("Events of:" + dateString + "\n
                blahblah");
            }
        });
        calendar.setValue(new Date(), true);
        eastPanel.add(new Label("Events:"));
        eastPanel.add(calendar);
        eastPanel.add(eventsLabel);
    }
```

Let's resolve the import errors:

Press *Ctrl+Shift+I*.

The **Fix All Imports** window should be exactly like the following screenshot:

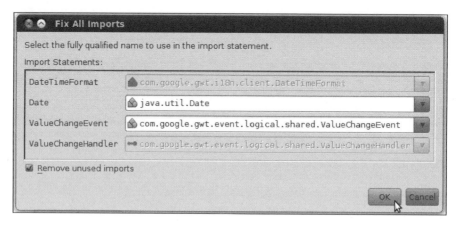

Click **OK** and save the File.

After the `createCalendar` method, add:

```
        private void createMenuBar() {
            Command command = new Command() {

                public void execute() {
                    Window.alert("Command executed.");
                }
            };
            for (int i = 0; i < 5; i++) {
                innerItem = new MenuBar(true);
```

```
        for (int j = 0; j < 5; j++) {
            innerItem.addItem("Inner Item" + j, command);
        }
        outerMenuBar.addItem("Menu" + i, innerItem);
    }
    textBox.setVisibleLength(150);
}
```

Let's resolve the import errors:

Press *Ctrl+Shift+I.*

The **Fix All Imports** Window should be exactly like the following screenshot:

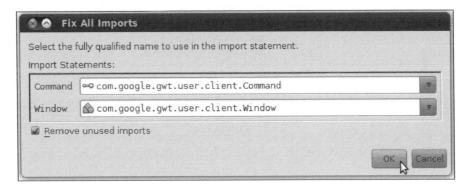

Click **OK** and save the File.

After the createMenuBar method, add:

```
    private void createButtonBehavior() {
        shareButton.addClickHandler(new ClickHandler() {

            @Override
            public void onClick(ClickEvent event) {
                HorizontalPanel blahPanelTemp = new
                HorizontalPanel();
                blahPanelTemp.add(new Image(HAPPY_FACE));
                blahPanelTemp.add(new Label(textBox.getText()));
                mainPanel.add(blahPanelTemp);
            }
        });
    }
```

Once again, resolve the import errors by pressing *Ctrl+Shift+I* and saving the File.

After `createButtonBehavior` method, add the code to create the UI:

```
private void createUI() {
    mainPanel.add(new Label("News:"));
    mainPanel.add(textBox);
    mainPanel.add(shareButton);
    HorizontalPanel blahPanel = new HorizontalPanel();
    blahPanel.add(new Image(ANGRY_FACE));
    blahPanel.add(new
       Label("BLAHBLAHBLAHBLAHBLAHBLAHBLAHBLAHBLAHBLAH!!!"));
    HorizontalPanel blahPanel2 = new HorizontalPanel();
    blahPanel2.add(new Image(HAPPY_FACE));
    blahPanel2.add(new
       Label("blahblahblahblahblahblahblahblahblah :)"));
    mainPanel.add(blahPanel);
    mainPanel.add(blahPanel2);
    dockLayoutPanel.addNorth(outerMenuBar, 2);
    dockLayoutPanel.addSouth(netbeansImage, 4);
    dockLayoutPanel.addWest(tree, 10);
    dockLayoutPanel.addEast(eastPanel, 15);
    dockLayoutPanel.add(mainPanel);
}
```

Save the file.

Finally, replace the available `onModuleLoad` method, in the beginning of the class, with:

```
public void onModuleLoad() {
    createTreeItem();
    createCalendar();
    createMenuBar();
    createButtonBehavior();
    createUI();
    RootLayoutPanel panel = RootLayoutPanel.get();
    panel.add(dockLayoutPanel);
}
```

Resolve the last import error by pressing *Ctrl+Shift+I* and then save the File.

How it works...

When the new GWT project is created, GWT4NB provides us with a complete project structure along with GWT-specific configuration files, GWT's entry point class, and a basic HTML page.

It is important to understand those files in order to proceed:

- ▶ `Main.gwt.xml`: This is the Module Descriptor. This file describes the configuration of the module, entry point classes, other inherited modules, and so on.
- ▶ `MainEntryPoint.java`: This is the GWT's equivalent of the `main()` method of a normal Java class. This class is always required to implement the EntryPoint interface.
- ▶ `welcomeGWT.html`: This is the host page. The host page is where the GWT application is started from.

With our Module Descriptor, it is possible to give themes to our application. This is done by either adding or just uncommenting the following line of code:

```
<inherits name='com.google.gwt.user.theme.standard.Standard'/>
```

We start our application by adding the necessary UI items as global variables. This is not the best practice, but for brevity's sake, we will use it anyway.

We use a `DockLayoutPanel` to structure the UI components of our application:

```
DockLayoutPanel dockLayoutPanel = new DockLayoutPanel(Unit.EM);
```

On the left-hand side, we add the TreeItem, with the `createTreeItem` methods, which is the menu where the users can find Updates, Photos, Videos, and so on. This is not dynamic since we do not have Updates, Photos, and Videos in our recipe.

Then the tree is added to the `dockLayoutPanel`:

```
dockLayoutPanel.addWest(tree, 10);
```

With the `createCalendar`, we add an Event Calendar to the right-hand side of the application. This is achieved by creating its own panel and passing the reference of the calendar itself. The calendar behavior can be triggered by clicking on each day or date.

The behavior is executed by using the following method:

```
public void onValueChange(ValueChangeEvent event)
```

Once clicked, the method changes the contents of a Label with the Events of that selected date.

At the top of the application window, we create and add a MenuBar. The MenuBar is dynamically created and each inner item of the menu has an event which pops up an alert window when clicked.

The share button is added inside the main panel. This button is responsible for retrieving the information from the Text Box, creating a new Horizontal Panel, adding an image and information to the Horizontal Panel, and finally adding this panel to the main panel.

This is all achieved by the `clickHandler` Inner Class and subsequent `onClick` method:

```
shareButton.addClickHandler(new ClickHandler() {
    public void onClick(ClickEvent event) {
//..code
    }
});
```

Adding an instance of a class, in our case the `ClickHandler`, is a common practice in UI development in Java, since it reduces the amount of code necessary for subclassing a specified handler and then implementing the method. Note that while this is convenient, if many handlers are used throughout the code, it is best to actually have a separate class for event handling.

The `createUI` method is responsible for assembling all of the component parts of the application and giving form to it.

At the end of this method, the dock panel receives the locations of each widget or panel created for that purpose.

Gluing all that together is the `onModuleLoad`, which creates all the UI components and adds them to the `RootLayoutPanel`, which binds together the Java class, the HTML page, and the Dock Layout Panel.

6
Using JavaFX

In this chapter, we will cover:

- ▶ Creating a JavaFX Project
- ▶ Build UI with NetBeans JavaFX Composer
- ▶ Connecting JavaFX Application to Web Service
- ▶ Connecting JavaFX Application to Database
- ▶ Application States in JavaFX

Introduction

JavaFX is a cross-platform runtime environment introduced by Sun Microsystems with the intent of building rich Internet applications across different kinds of devices. It is not only intended to be used on Desktop, but also to be deployed on set-top boxes, cell phones, TVs, and more.

With the upcoming release of JavaFX 2.0, Oracle will be porting all of the APIs that once were available under JavaFX Script into the Java language. This will make JavaFX more familiar to those who already know Java. The new version will also make it easier to 'talk' to other dynamic languages that run on top of the VM, such as Groovy and JRuby.

Since Oracle has removed the JavaFX support from NetBeans 7 we will need to use version 6.9 or older. Version 7 does not include libraries, visual editor and other features required for the creation and maintainence of JavaFx projects. Simply head on to NetBeans website and download 6.9 or 6.9.1.

```
http://netbeans.org/community/releases/69/
```

If you wish to learn more about JavaFX, please visit:

```
http://www.javafx.com/
```

A combination of JavaFX Script and Java is used to build visually rich, interesting applications. NetBeans IDE provides a set of plugins that ease the development of such applications.

To get a glimpse of what JavaFX is capable of doing, please visit the sample applications at:

```
http://javafx.com/samples/
```

In this chapter, we will configure the IDE to work with JavaFX, learn how to use the JavaFX composer, create a small app that connects to (and retrieves information from) Facebook, create another app to connect to a database, and learn about JavaFX states.

Creating a JavaFX Project

In this recipe, we will install the plugins required for working with JavaFX and also create our first project that will serve as the basis for some of the next recipes.

Getting ready

There are two options to start working with NetBeans:

First, it is possible to download the specific IDE for JavaFX from the NetBeans site. Just go to the download section and select the JavaFX version.

Second, if NetBeans is already installed on your machine, simply open the IDE, click on **Tools** and **Plugins**, then select the following components:

- ► JavaFX Bind Inspector (if Bind Inspector is not shown, click on the name header and sort by name first)
- ► JavaFX Composer
- ► JavaFX Kit

And click **Install**.

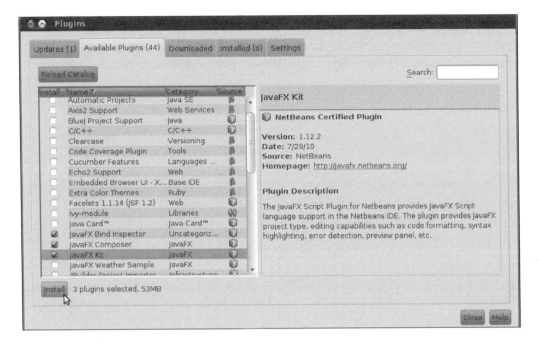

Follow the steps of the **NetBeans IDE Installer** and accept a License Agreement. The NetBeans plugins will be downloaded and installed automatically. At the end of this process, the IDE will ask if you wish to restart the IDE, choose **Restart IDE Now** and click **Finish**.

When the IDE completes the installation of the plugins, it restarts and after that we are ready to go.

How to do it...

To Create a New Project:

1. Click on **File** and then **New Project** (or press *Ctrl+Shift+N*).

2. **Choose Project**: In the **New Project** window, on the **Categories** side choose **JavaFX** and on **Projects** side select **JavaFX Desktop Business Application**, and click **Next>**.

3. Under **Project Name**, enter **JavaFXApp**, leave all the other fields with their default values and click **Finish**.

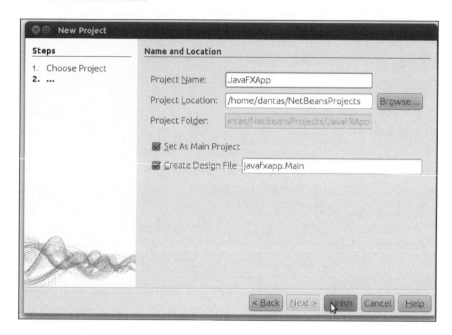

How it works...

NetBeans, in conjunction with JavaFX SDK, creates a project structure, assigns the necessary libraries for the project to work, and creates `Main.fx`.

`Main.fx` is the main class that we will be building our future applications on, and where we will place the components from the JavaFX Palette.

Note that due to NetBeans JavaFX Composer, the `Main.fx` is already created and presented with the visual Components Palette and the design mode on.

Below is the file structure of our newly created project:

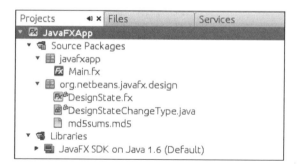

There's more...

Feeling curious about JavaFX?

Available samples

The JavaFX SDK provides samples of what can be done with JavaFX.

To check them out:

1. Create a New Project, this can be achieved by clicking on **File** and then **New Project** (or pressing *Ctrl+Shift+N*).

2. **Choose Project**: In the **New Project** window, on the **Categories** side, expand the **Samples** node and choose **JavaFX** and on **Projects side** there are many project samples.

The list of available examples is extensive and will cover pretty much all the needed functionality and APIs that a developer might need.

Examples of these projects are:

- ▶ Drag and Drop example
- ▶ Google Image Search
- ▶ JDBC Address Book
- ▶ RSS Reader

And many more.

Just open one and start learning more about JavaFX.

Build UI with NetBeans JavaFX Composer

Building JavaFX applications with NetBeans is a top-notch experience. It is incredible to see how effortless coding with this tool actually is.

NetBeans JavaFX Composer provides a Palette with a wide range of readily-available components, making it possible to construct well-crafted and precise UIs with a simple drag-and-drop.

Along with the known windows, such as **Navigator** and **Editor**, the **JavaFX Composer** brings new windows: **Design Area** (similar to the one present when building Swing applications) and the **States editor**.

Getting ready

A JavaFX Desktop Business Application project must be created or imported. We will use the project created in the previous recipe.

If unsure how to proceed, take a look at our first recipe in this chapter; there you will find all the necessary information.

With all of the settings and projects in place, let's continue.

How to do it...

With the `JavaFXApp` open:

1. With `Main.fx` open and with the **Design** mode on, click on the resolution drop-down and select **Desktop 800x600**.

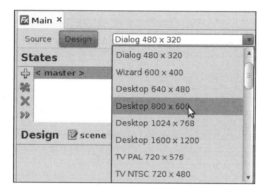

2. From the Palette, add the following components from under the **Controls** section:
    - ❑ 2 List Views
    - ❑ 2 Labels
    - ❑ 1 Progress Bar
    - ❑ 1 Button

After adding all of those components, take some time to design the application like this:

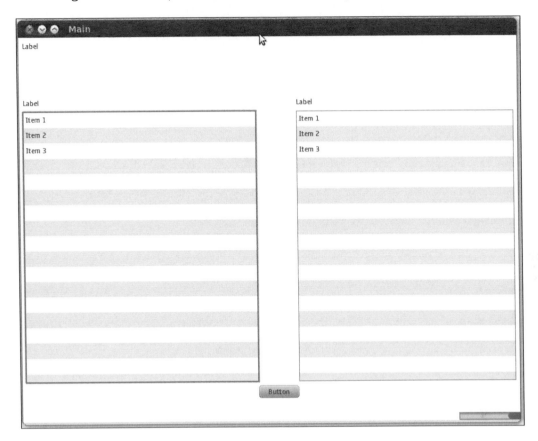

To arrange the components in each place, drag-and-drop a component to the desired location. It is also possible to expand each window by placing the mouse cursor on the corner and then dragging it.

How it works...

NetBeans does the hard work of creating, declaring, and designing all of the chosen components that were selected from the Palette.

To check how this is done, we need to take a look at the source code.

This is possible by toggling the **Source** button placed on top of the Editor. Once the button is pressed, the editor changes from **Design** mode into **Source** mode.

The Generated Code block is where all of the code that was built by NetBeans is placed. NetBeans creates this non-editable block so developers can be sure that no unintended consequence can come by modifying what was created by the IDE.

To see what was generated by the IDE, press the expand signal for the Generated Code:

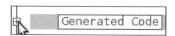

There's more...

Here is how to change the application title and better emphasize the content by changing the fonts in your application.

Changing the name of the application

To name our application, we need to click on the **Source** button inside the code editor.

In **Source** mode, the editor shows the `Main.fx` code. Search for the line that contains:

Title: `Main`

Inside the function `run(): Void`.

Then replace `Main` with `MyBook` and run the application.

Changing the font of the labels

To change the font of some of our labels using NetBeans JavaFX Composer, we need to have the editor in the **Design** mode.

Click on the **Design** button.

Then on the **Navigator** window, expand the **Design File** and **scene**, and click on **label**.

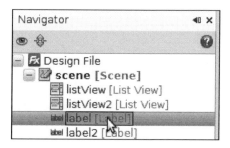

With **label** selected, navigate to the **Properties** window and click on the green plus sign to add a new font.

After clicking on the green sign, change **Size** to **24**. After changing the **Size** value, the label will be shown much bigger.

Now let's change the contents of each label:

1. Simply select the desired label in the code editor in the **Design** mode.
2. In the **Properties** window of that specific Label, change the **Text** property.

Our App should look like this now:

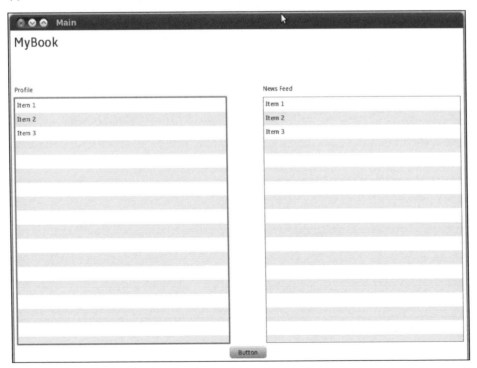

Connecting JavaFX Application to Web Service

Nowadays, if a developer is building an application, there are chances that the need to access a server or web service will arise in some form or another.

Either updates or just data being transmitted over the Internet might give developers the chill merely thinking about the complexity of handling connections, data parsing, and numerous controls. With NetBeans and JavaFX, many of those headaches are no longer a problem.

In this recipe, we will connect our application to Facebook and retrieve some data from the news feed and profile.

Getting ready

To continue with this recipe, NetBeans and the plugins set of JavaFX must be installed.

Also, a JavaFX Desktop Business Application project must be created or imported. We will use the project created in the previous recipe.

If unsure how to proceed in any of these steps, take a look at *Creating a JavaFX Project* and *Build UI with NetBeans JavaFX Composer* recipes in this chapter to find all of the information required.

From Facebook we will need to access the following links:

`http://developers.facebook.com/docs/reference/rest/status.get/`

`http://developers.facebook.com/docs/reference/rest/stream.get/`

The above links lead to the Facebook **REST** (**Representational State Transfer**) API. REST is an architectural style which is built on top of HTTP and XML, where an application will be responsible for reading and parsing data from the provided XML.

On both pages, find the **Test Console** and click on:

`https://api.facebook.com/method/stream.get?`

`access_token=...`

And

`https://api.facebook.com/method/status.get?`

`access_token=...`

Below is a screenshot of what you will find in Facebook's developer page and where to click:

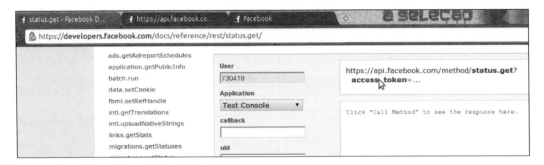

New windows will open, displaying the URLs that are going to be used to fetch the information. Copy both the URLs somewhere and keep them for later.

Both windows will provide the user with the access tokens for the information being requested. In our example, the tokens are valid for both status and stream from Facebook.

Note that some browsers might not properly display the above URLs; instead, they ask the user to download a file. If that is the case, please use another browser to check the link properly.

With all of the settings and projects in place, let's continue.

How to do it...

Following are the steps on how to add an HTTP Data Source for Facebook status message.

With the `JavaFXApp` project open:

1. Navigate to the **Palette** and on the Data Sources subsection, drag-and-drop an **HTTP Data Source**.
2. Copy the `status.get` token generated by Facebook. (We will use it shortly).
3. Configure the **Data Source Customizer** dialog as shown in the following screenshot:

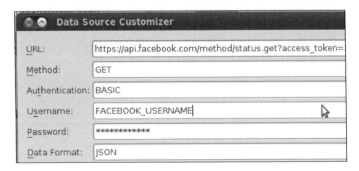

4. Click on **Fetch Data** (bear in mind that the Facebook username is the user's e-mail).

5. Expand the **aRecordSet**, then expand **aRecord**, select **message**, and click the **Add** button.

6. The input dialog pops up asking for **Filter Expression**. Leave the default and press **OK**.

7. Back on the **Data Source Customizer**, click **OK**.

Now we add an HTTP Data Source for Facebook News Stream:

1. Navigate to the **Palette** and drag-and-drop another **HTTP Data Source**.

2. This time, copy the `stream.get` token.

3. Expand the **aRecordSet**, then expand **aRecord**, select the **posts** node, and click the **Add** button.

4. The input dialog pops up asking for **Filter Expression**. Leave the default and press **OK**.

5. Back on the **Data Source Customizer**, click **OK**.

To bind a HTTP Source to the correct List Views Profile:

1. In the **Navigator** window, expand **Design File**, then expand **scene**, and select **listView**.

2. Then in the **Properties** window, click on the **Items** button.

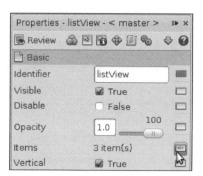

3. On the top-right corner of the new pop-up, click on **Bind**.

4. Under Components, select **httpDataSource["message"]**.

5. Under **Properties**, select **All Records**.

6. After following these steps, the **List View Binding** dialog will look like this:

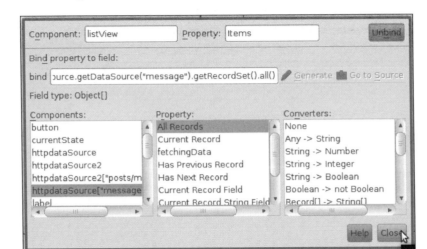

7. Back in the **Properties** window, we need to add a **Cell Factory**.

8. Click on the green plus sign related to the **Cell Factory**.

9. In the **Properties** window, click on the **Text** button and clear the text under **Bind.**

10. Then, under **Components**, select **listCell**.

11. Under **Properties**, select **item**.

12. Under **Converters**, select **Record**.

13. Append to the following code to the end of the bind text:

```
.getString("message")
```

14. Click **close**.

We will then bind the HTTP Source to the correct List Views Status:

1. In the **Navigator** window, expand the **Design File**, then expand **scene**, and select **listView2**.

2. Then, on the **Properties** window, click on the items button.

3. On the top-right corner of the new pop-up, click on **Bind**.

4. Under Components, select **httpDataSource2["posts"]**.

5. Under **Properties**, select **All Records**.

6. Under **Converters**, select **Record[] | String []**.

7. Append the following code to the end of the bind text:

    ```
    for(record in httpdataSource2.getDataSource("posts/message").
    getRecordSet().all()) record.getString("name")
    ```

8. Click on **Close**.

Save the file and click on **Run the Main Project**.

How it works...

Facebook allows developers to access information through their RESTful API. To access that information, we will need to implement the HTTP Data Source, configured to parse a JSON feed.

After configuring the Data Source Customizer, it is very useful to click on Fetch Data. This way we know that the connection between the Data Source and Facebook is working.

NetBeans makes it very easy to bind JavaFX components by simply clicking a few buttons. Through the Binder, it is possible to attach our HTTP Data Sources to the list views, and choose which kind of format we will be displaying the information in.

Connecting JavaFX Application to Database

Another common scenario is connecting an application to a database.

In this recipe, we will see how to create a JavaFX Desktop application with form and index buttons.

Getting ready

To continue with this recipe, NetBeans and the set of plugins that bundle JavaFX must be installed.

If unsure how to proceed, please refer to the recipe, *Creating a JavaFX Project*, specifically the *Getting ready* section.

We also need JavaDB Database running.

To do this:

1. Navigate to the **Services** window.

2. Expand the **Database** section.

3. Right-click on **jdbc:derby://localhost:1527/sample [app on APP]** and select **Connect...**.

4. The following screenshot shows the active connection to **JavaDB**:

How to do it...

We need to create a New Project:

1. Click on **File** and then **New Project** (or Press *Ctrl+Shift+N*).

2. **Choose Project**: In the **New Project** window, on the **Categories** side, choose **JavaFX** and on the **Projects** side, select **JavaFX Desktop Business Application**. Then click **Next**.

3. Under **Project Name**, enter **DesktopDBJavaFXApp**, leave all the other fields with their default values and click **Finish**.

4. On the **Palette** window, navigate to **Data Sources** and drag-and-drop the **JDBC Data Source** to Main.fx.

5. On the **Data Source Customizer** dialog, click on **Browse...**.

6. Select **jdbc:derby://localhost:1527/sample [app on APP]** and click **OK.**

7. Then click the **Create...** button.

8. On the **Create SQL Query** dialog, select **CUSTOMER** under **tables**, and click **OK**.

9. Back on the **Create SQL Query** dialog, click on **Fetch Data** to check that everything is fine, then click **OK.**

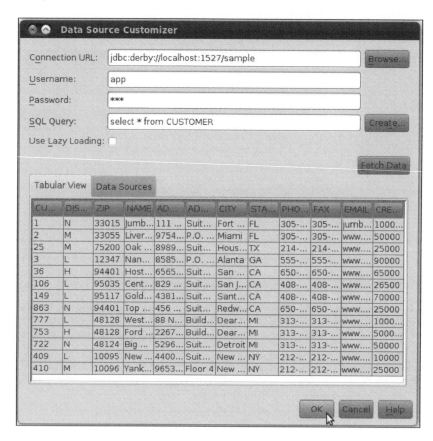

10. Navigate to the **Palette** window and under the **Templates** section, drag-and-drop the **Desktop Form** component inside `Main.fx`.

11. On the **Customize Template** dialog, click on the **Data Source** drop-down and select **jdbcDataSource**, click on **Fetch** to see all the fields that are going to be added, and then click **OK**.

12. On the **Palette** window, under the **Templates** section, drag-and-drop **Index Buttons**.

13. On the **Customize Template** dialog, click on the **Indexed Component** drop-down, select **jdbcDataSource**, and click **OK**.

14. We need to add JavaDB JARs to our project. Right-click on **DesktopDBJavaFXApp** and select **Properties**.

15. Click on **Libraries** and then **Add JAR/Folder**.

16. Navigate to the JavaDB installation folder inside the JDK 6 folder, and select `derby.jar` and `derbyclient.jar`.

17. Click **OK**.

Save the file and click on **Run the Main Project**.

How it works...

The **JDBC Data Source** is responsible for connecting/fetching/updating our database. This is done by executing SQL queries in the background.

These actions are transparent for the developer since the **JDBC Data Source** is responsible for abstracting all of the work and only lets the developer customize the settings through the GUI.

The **Create SQL Query** dialog is used in our case, to perform a selection of all of the entries from the `Customer` table.

Different SQL queries could be used in conjunction with the **Data Source Customizer**, but as we only want to display the data, this is the query used in the recipe.

After configuring the connection to the Database, we will need to actually bind the connection to some component.

The `Desktop Form` component is responsible for showing the data. When customizing it, we add as our Data Source the `jdbcDataSource`, which we have configured with the `Customer` table. This will provide the application with all the data, presented in a well-formatted manner.

For our app to work, we need to add the Java DB JARs otherwise the app won't behave correctly.

Application States in JavaFX

JavaFX Application States are very self-descriptive. In each different state, a JavaFX application or component holds a set of characteristics. By transitioning between different states, it is possible to add motion or behavior.

In this recipe, we will use states to change the background color of our application. It might not be the most useful use of states, but it exemplifies correctly what can be achieved.

Getting ready

To continue with this recipe, NetBeans and the set of plugins that bundle JavaFX must be installed.

If unsure how to proceed, please refer to the recipe *Creating a JavaFX Project*, specifically the *Getting ready* section section.

For this recipe, we will be continuing with the Project created in the previous recipe.

We also need the JavaDB Database running. If unsure how to proceed, please refer to the previous recipe, where all the information required to setup and run Java DB is in place.

With NetBeans configured and our project in place, let's start the recipe.

How to do it...

First we need to add states.

Open `Main.fx` in the **Design** mode:

1. On the **States** section, click on the green plus sign.

2. The **Add State** dialog pops up, under **State Name**, type **First**.
3. Then click again on the green plus sign and on the **Add State** dialog, type **Second**.

We will need to change the Second state. Click on the **Second** state under the States editor:

1. Click on an empty space in our `Main.fx` file.
2. Navigate to the **Properties** window and click on the green plus sign related to **Background Fill**, then select **Color**, and choose any color you like when the **Choose Color** dialog pops up.

We will then start coding the state Transition:

1. Under the **State** editor, click on the **First** state.
2. Select the **index buttons** inside `Main.fx`, navigate to the **Properties** window, and under **action**, click on **101 button** (101 is only shown if the *Connecting JavaFX Application to Database* was used as base for this recipe, otherwise no 101 text is shown).

3. On the pop-up, click on **Use specified function name** and click **Generate.**

4. Inside the **indexNextButtonAction** function, add the following:

```
jdbcdataSource.getRecordSet().next();
currentState.nextWrapped();
```

Save the file and click on **Run Main Project**.

How it works...

When we create the First and the Second state, both states have **Background Fill** for `Main.fx` set as white.

For Second state, we then set the **Background Fill** to the color of our choice but do not have a way to add transition to that state.

So to add the State transition, we need to override the code generated for the index button by the IDE, since this is where we are interacting with the application.

So, for we ask the IDE to generate another function. In that function, we ask `jdbcdataSource` to retrieve the next record in line, and then we iterate the `currentState` variable, transitioning to the other state.

7
EJB Application

In this chapter, we will cover:

- ▶ Creating an EJB project
- ▶ Adding JPA support
- ▶ Creating Stateless Session Bean
- ▶ Creating Stateful Session Bean
- ▶ Sharing a service through Web Service
- ▶ Creating a Web Service client

Introduction

Enterprise Java Beans (EJB) is a framework of server-side components that encapsulates business logic.

These components adhere to strict specifications on how they should behave. This ensures that vendors who wish to implement EJB-compliant code must follow conventions, protocols, and classes ensuring portability.

The EJB components are then deployed in EJB containers, also called **application servers**, which manage persistence, transactions, and security on behalf of the developer.

If you wish to learn more about EJBs, visit `http://jcp.org/en/jsr/detail?id=318` or `https://www.packtpub.com/developer-guide-for-ejb3/book`.

For our EJB application to run, we will need the application servers.

Application servers are responsible for implementing the EJB specifications and creating the perfect environment for our EJBs to run in.

Some of the capabilities supported by EJB and enforced by Application Servers are:

- ▶ Remote access
- ▶ Transactions
- ▶ Security Scalability

NetBeans 6.9, or higher, supports the new Java EE 6 platform, making it the only IDE so far to bring the full power of EJB 3.1 to a simple IDE interface for easy development.

NetBeans makes it easy to develop an EJB application and deploy on different Application Servers without the need to over-configure and mess with different configuration files. It's as easy as a project node right-click.

Creating EJB project

In this recipe, we will see how to create an EJB project using the wizards provided by NetBeans.

Getting ready

It is required to have NetBeans with Java EE support installed to continue with this recipe.

If this particular NetBeans version is not available in your machine, then you can download it from `http://download.netbeans.org`.

There are two application servers in this installation package, Apache Tomcat or GlassFish, and either one can be chosen, but at least one is necessary.

In this recipe, we will use the GlassFish version that comes together with NetBeans 7.0 installation package.

How to do it...

1. Lets create a new project by either clicking **File** and then **New Project**, or by pressing *Ctrl+Shift+N*.
2. In the **New Project** window, in the categories side, choose **Java Web** and in **Projects side**, select **WebApplication**, then click **Next**.
3. In **Name and Location**, under Project Name, enter **EJBApplication**.
4. Tick the **Use Dedicated Folder for Storing Libraries** option box.
5. Now either type the folder path or select one by clicking on **browse**.
6. After choosing the folder, we can proceed by clicking **Next**.

7. In **Server and Settings**, under **Server**, choose **GlassFish Server 3.1**.

8. Tick **Enable Contexts and Dependency Injection**.

9. Leave the other values with their default values and click **Finish**.

The new project structure is created.

How it works...

NetBeans creates a complete file structure for our project.

It automatically configures the compiler and test libraries and creates the GlassFish deployment descriptor.

The deployment descriptor filename specific for the GlassFish web server is `glassfish-web.xml`.

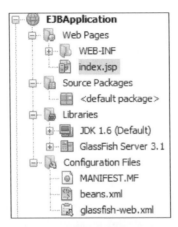

Adding JPA support

The **Java Persistence API** (**JPA**) is one of the frameworks that equips Java with object/relational mapping. Within JPA, a query language is provided that supports the developers abstracting the underlying database.

With the release of JPA 2.0, there are many areas that were improved, such as:

► Domain Modeling

► EntityManager

► Query interfaces

► JPA query language and others

We are not going to study the inner workings of JPA in this recipe. If you wish to know more about JPA, visit `http://jcp.org/en/jsr/detail?id=317` or

`http://download.oracle.com/javaee/5/tutorial/doc/bnbqa.html`.

NetBeans provides very good support for enabling your application to quickly create entities annotated with JPA.

In this recipe, we will see how to configure your application to use JPA. We will continue to expand the previously-created project.

Getting ready

We will use GlassFish Server in this recipe since it is the only server that supports Java EE 6 at the moment.

We also need to have Java DB configured. GlassFish already includes a copy of Java DB in its installation folder. Another source of installed Java DB is the JDK installation directory. If you wish to learn how to configure Java DB, please refer to *Chapter 4, JDBC and NetBeans*.

It is not necessary to build on top of the previous recipe, but it is imperative to have a database schema. Feel free to create your own entities by following the steps presented in this recipe.

How to do it...

1. Right-click on **EJBApplication** node and select **New Entity Classes from Database...**.
2. In **Database Tables**: Under **Data Source**, select **jdbc/sample** and let the IDE initialize Java DB.
3. When **Available Tables** is populated, select **MANUFACTURER**, click **Add**, and then click **Next**.

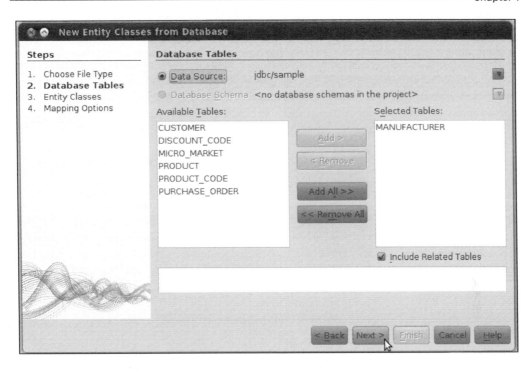

4. In **Entity Classes**: leave all the fields with their default values and only in **Package**, enter entities and click **Finish**.

How it works...

NetBeans then imports and creates our Java class from the database schema, in our case the `Manufacturer.java` file placed under the entities package.

Besides that, NetBeans makes it easy to import and start using the entity straightaway. Many of the most common queries, for example find by name, find by zip, and find all, are already built into the class itself.

The JPA queries, which are akin to normal SQL queries, are defined in the entity class itself. Listed below are some of the queries defined in the entity class `Manufacturer.java`:

```
@Entity
@Table(name = "MANUFACTURER")
@NamedQueries({
    @NamedQuery(name = "Manufacturer.findAll", query = "SELECT m FROM
Manufacturer m"),
    @NamedQuery(name = "Manufacturer.findByManufacturerId", query
= "SELECT m FROM Manufacturer m WHERE m.manufacturerId =
:manufacturerId"),
```

The `@Entity` annotation defines that this class, `Manufacturer.java`, is an entity and when followed by the `@Table` annotation, which has a name parameter, points out the table in the Database where the information is stored.

The `@NamedQueries` annotation is the place where all the NetBeans-generated JPA queries are stored. There can be as many `@NamedQueries` as the developer feels necessary. One of the NamedQueries we are using in our example is named `Manufacturer.findAll`, which is a simple select query. When invoked, the query is translated to:

```
SELECT m FROM Manufacturer m
```

On top of that, NetBeans implements the equals, hashCode, and toString methods. Very useful if the entities need to be used straight away with some collections, such as HashMap.

Below is the NetBeans-generated code for both hashCode and the toString methods:

```
    @Override
    public int hashCode() {
        int hash = 0;
        hash += (manufacturerId != null ? manufacturerId.hashCode() :
0);
        return hash;
    }


    @Override
    public boolean equals(Object object) {
        // TODO: Warning - this method won't work in the case the id
fields are not set
        if (!(object instanceof Manufacturer)) {
            return false;
        }
        Manufacturer other = (Manufacturer) object;
        if ((this.manufacturerId == null && other.manufacturerId
!= null) || (this.manufacturerId != null && !this.manufacturerId.
equals(other.manufacturerId))) {
            return false;
        }
        return true;
    }
```

NetBeans also creates a `persistence.xml` and provides a Visual Editor, simplifying the management of different Persistence Units (in case our project needs to use more than one); thereby making it possible to manage the `persistence.xml` without even touching the XML code. A persistence unit, or `persistence.xml`, is the configuration file in JPA which is placed under the configuration files, when the NetBeans view is in Projects mode. This file defines the data source and what name the persistence unit has in our example:

```
<persistence-unit name="EJBApplicationPU" transaction-type="JTA">
  <jta-data-source>jdbc/sample</jta-data-source>
  <properties/>
</persistence-unit>
```

The `persistence.xml` is placed in the configuration folder, when using the Projects view. In our example, our persistence unit name is `EJBApplicationPU`, using the `jdbc/sample` as the data source.

To add more PUs, click on the **Add** button that is placed on the uppermost right corner of the Persistence Visual Editor.

This is an example of adding another PU to our project:

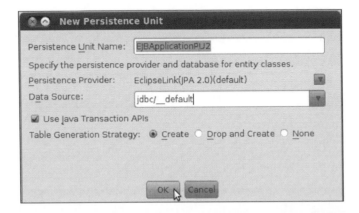

Creating Stateless Session Bean

A Session Bean encapsulates business logic in methods, which in turn are executed by a client. This way, the business logic is separated from the client.

Stateless Session Beans do not maintain state. This means that when a client invokes a method in a Stateless bean, the bean is ready to be reused by another client. The information stored in the bean is generally discarded when the client stops accessing the bean.

This type of bean is mainly used for persistence purposes, since persistence does not require a conversation with the client.

It is not in the scope of this recipe to learn how Stateless Beans work in detail. If you wish to learn more, please visit:

`http://jcp.org/en/jsr/detail?id=318`

or

`https://www.packtpub.com/developer-guide-for-ejb3/book`

In this recipe, we will see how to use NetBeans to create a Stateless Session Bean that retrieves information from the database, passes through a servlet and prints this information on a page that is created on-the-fly by our servlet.

Getting ready

It is required to have NetBeans with Java EE support installed to continue with this recipe.

If this particular NetBeans version is not available in your machine, please visit http://download.netbeans.org.

We will use the GlassFish Server in this recipe since it is the only Server that supports Java EE 6 at the moment.

We also need to have Java DB configured. GlassFish already includes a copy of Java DB in its installation folder. If you wish to learn how to configure Java DB refer to the *Chapter 4, JDBC and NetBeans*.

It is possible to follow the steps on this recipe without the previous code, but for better understanding we will continue to build on the top of the previous recipes source code.

How to do it...

1. Right-click on **EJBApplication** node and select **New and Session Bean....**
2. For **Name and Location**: Name the EJB as **ManufacturerEJB**.
3. Under **Package**, enter **beans**.
4. Leave **Session Type** as **Stateless**.
5. Leave **Create Interface** with nothing marked and click **Finish**.

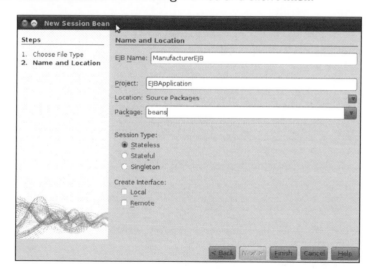

Here are the steps for us to create business methods:

1. Open ManufacturerEJB and inside the class body, enter:

```
@PersistenceUnit
EntityManagerFactory emf;

public List findAll(){
  return emf.createEntityManager().createNamedQuery("Manufacturer.
findAll").getResultList();
}
```

2. Press *Ctrl+Shift+I* to resolve the following imports:

```
java.util.List;
javax.persistence.EntityManagerFactory;
javax.persistence.PersistenceUnit;
```

Creating the Servlet:

1. Right-click on the **EJBApplication** node and select **New and Servlet....**

2. For **Name and Location**: Name the servlet as **ManufacturerServlet**.

3. Under **package**, enter **servlets**.

4. Leave all the other fields with their default values and click **Next**.

5. For **Configure Servlet Deployment**: Leave all the default values and click **Finish**.

With the **ManufacturerServlet** open:

After the class declaration and before the `processRequest` method, add:

```
@EJB
ManufacturerEJB manufacturerEJB;
```

Then inside the **processRequest** method, first line after the `try` statement, add:

```
List<Manufacturer> l = manufacturerEJB.findAll();
```

Remove the /* TODO output your page here and also */.

And finally replace:

```
out.println("<h1>Servlet ManufacturerServlet at " + request.
getContextPath () + "</h1>");
```

With:

```
for(int i = 0; i < 10; i++ )
  out.println("<b>City</b> " + l.get(i).getCity() + ", <b>State</b> " +
l.get(i).getState() +"<br>" );
```

Resolve all the import errors and save the file.

How it works...

To execute the code produced in this recipe, right-click on the **EJBApplication** node and select **Run**.

When the browser launches append to the end of the URL/ManufacturerServlet, hit *Enter*.

Our application will return City and State names.

One of the coolest features in Java EE 6 is that usage of `web.xml` can be avoided if annotating the servlet. The following code does exactly that:

```
@WebServlet(name="ManufacturerServlet", urlPatterns={"/
ManufacturerServlet"})
```

Since we are working on Java EE 6, our Stateless bean does not need the daunting work of creating interfaces, the `@Stateless` annotation takes care of that, making it easier to develop EJBs.

We then add the persistence unit, represented by the EntityManagerFactory and inserted by the `@PersistenceUnit` annotation.

Finally we have our business method that is used from the servlet. The `findAll` method uses one of the named queries from our entity to fetch information from the database.

Creating Stateful Session Beans

If Stateless Session Beans do not maintain state, it is easy to guess what Stateful Session Beans do. Yes, they maintain the state.

When a client invokes a method in a stateful bean, the variables (state) of that request are kept in the memory by the bean. When more requests come in, the container makes sure that the same bean is used for the same client. This type of bean is useful when multiple requests are required and several steps are necessary for completing a task.

Stateful Beans also enjoy the ease of development introduced by Java EE 6, meaning that they can be created by annotating a POJO with `@Stateful`.

It is not in the scope of this recipe to learn how Stateful Beans work in detail. If you wish to learn more, please visit:

```
http://jcp.org/en/jsr/detail?id=318
```

Or

```
https://www.packtpub.com/developer-guide-for-ejb3/book
```

In this recipe, we will see how to use NetBeans to create a stateful session bean that holds a counter of how many times a request for a method was executed.

Getting ready

Please find the software requirements and configuration instructions for this recipe in the first *Getting ready* section of this chapter.

This recipe builds on the sources of the previous recipes.

How to do it...

1. Right-click on the EJBApplication node and select **New Session Bean...**.
2. For **Name** and **Location**: Name the EJB as **CounterManufacturerEJB**.
3. Under **Package**, enter **beans**.
4. Mark **Session Type** as **Stateful**.
5. Leave **Create Interface** with nothing marked and click **Finish**.

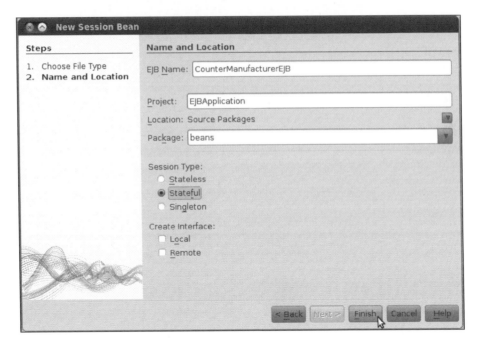

Creating the business method

With **CounterManufacturerEJB** open, add the following variable:

```
private int counter = 0;
```

Then right-click inside the class body and select **Insert Code...** (or press *Alt+Insert*) and select **Add Business Method...**.

When the **Add Business Method...** window opens:

1. **Name** it as **counter** and for **Return Type**, enter **String**.
2. Click **OK.**

Replace the code inside the counter method with:

```
counter++;
return ""+counter;
```

Save the file.

Open `ManufacturerServlet` and after the class declaration and before the `processRequest` method:

1. Right-click and select **Insert Code...** or press *Alt+Insert*.
2. Select **Call Enterprise Bean...**.
3. In the **Call Enterprise Bean** window, expand the EJB Application node.
4. Select **CounterManufacturerEJB** and click **OK**.

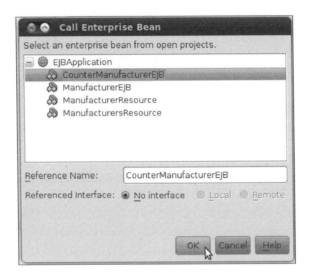

Below we see how the bean is injected using annotation:

```
@EJB
CounterManufacturerEJB counterManufacturerEJB;
```

Resolve the import errors by pressing *Ctrl+Shift+I*.

Then add to the process request:

```
out.println("<b>Number of times counter was accessed<b>   " +
counterManufacturerEJB.counter() + "<br><br>" );
```

Save the file.

How it works...

NetBeans presents the user with a very easy-to-use wizard for creating beans. As with the stateless bean, we are presented with the different options for creating a bean.

This time we select the Stateful Bean. When clicking **Finish**, the IDE will create the EJB POJO class, place it in the beans package, and annotate, with `@Stateful`, the class signifying that we have created a Stateful Session Bean.

We then proceed to add the logic in our EJB. Through another wizard, NetBeans makes it easy to add a business method. After pressing *Alt+Insert*, we are presented with the choices of what can be done in that context. After adding the code, we are ready to integrate our EJB with the servlet.

Again, pressing *Alt+Insert* comes in handy when we want to create a reference to our EJB. After the correct bean is selected in the **Call Enterprise Bean** window, NetBeans creates the code:

```
CounterManufacturerEJB counterManufacturerEJB =
lookupCounterManufacturerEJBBean();
```

And also:

```
    private CounterManufacturerEJB lookupCounterManufacturerEJBBean()
{
        try {
            Context c = new InitialContext();
            return (CounterManufacturerEJB) c.lookup("java:global/
EJBApplication/CounterManufacturerEJB!beans.CounterManufacturerEJB");
        } catch (NamingException ne) {
            Logger.getLogger(getClass().getName()).log(Level.SEVERE,
"exception caught", ne);
            throw new RuntimeException(ne);
        }
    }
```

This boatload of code is created by the IDE and enables the developer to fine-tune things like logging over exceptions and other customizations. In fact, this is the way that EJB was called prior to annotations being introduced to Java EE. The method is simply calling the **application server context** with the lookup method, along with the **Remote Method Invocation** (**RMI**) naming conventions used to define our EJB and assign the reference to the object itself.

Notice that all this code could be simplified to:

```
@EJB
CounterManufacturerEJB counterManufacturerEJB;
```

But we tried to show how much liberty and options the developer has in NetBeans.

There's more...

Disabling GlassFish alive sessions.

GlassFish and sessions

To keep sessions alive in our Application Server GlassFish, we need to navigate to the Services window:

1. There we will need to expand the **Servers** node.

2. Right-click on **GlassFish** and select **Properties**.

3. Click on **Preserve Sessions Across Redeployment** if you do not want this feature.

This option preserves the HTTP sessions even when GlassFish has been redeployed. If the data has been stored in a session, it will be available next time a redeployment occurs.

Sharing a service through Web Service

Web services are APIs which, in the case of this recipe, access some data over a network from any platform and using any programming language.

In the world of cloud computing, web services have become an increasingly popular way for companies to let developers create applications using their data. A good example of this is Twitter. Thanks to exposition of Twitter data through web services, it has been possible to create numerous Twitter clients on virtually all platforms. In this recipe, we will create a web service that returns information from a database table; we will see that this information can be transferred either in XML or **JavaScript Object Notation** (**JSON**) format. JSON provides the user with data access simplicity, when compared to XML, since it does not need a bunch of tags and nested tags to work *Getting ready*

It is required to have NetBeans with Java EE support installed to continue with this recipe.

If this particular NetBeans version is not available in your machine, please visit:

`http://netbeans.org`

We will use the GlassFish Server in this recipe since it is the only server that supports Java EE 6 at the moment.

We also need to have Java DB configured. GlassFish already includes a copy of Java DB in its installation folder. If you wish to learn how to configure Java DB, refer to *Chapter 4, JDBC and NetBeans*.

It is possible to create this recipe if an existing database schema and an EJB application exists. However, for the sake of brevity, we will use the sources from the previous recipes.

How to do it...

Right-click on the **EJBApplication** node, select **New** then **Other** then **Web Services and RESTFul Web Services from Entity Class**....

1. For **Entity Classes**: On **Available Entity classes**, select **Manufacturer**, click **Add**, and click **Next**.

2. For **Generated Classes**: Leave all the fields with their default values and click **Finish**.

A new dialog, **REST Resources Configuration**, pops-up; select the first option and click **OK**.

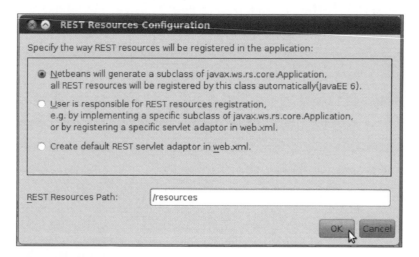

How it works...

The REST resources configuration asks the user which way the RESTful resources should be accessed, presenting the user with three different options. We have chosen to use `javax.ws.rs.core.Application` because it is the standard in Java EE 6 and, thus, increases the portability of the application, instead of the `web.xml` option. The second option allows the developer to code their way through registering the resources and choosing the service path.

To take a look at the generated files, expand the service package. Two java files are present: `AbstractFacade.java and ManufacturerFacadeREST.java`.

Opening the `ManufacturerFacadeREST.java` will show that this file is actually a stateless EJB created by the IDE that is used to interface with the database and retrieve information from it.

NetBeans also automatically generates a converter for our ManufacturerResource. This converter is used for creating a resource representation from the corresponding entity instance. Those classes can be found in the converter package.

There's more...

Using NetBeans to test the web services.

Testing the web service

Now that we have created a RESTful web service, we need to know if everything is working correctly or not.

To test our web service, right-click `EJBApplication` and select **Test RESTful Web Service**. NetBeans will be launched; deploy our application in GlassFish and then point the browser to the web service.

When the Test RESTful Web Service page opens, click on the **Test** button on the right side.

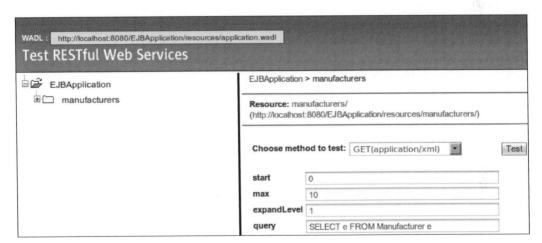

Upon clicking **Test**, the test request is sent to the server. The results can be seen in the response section.

Under **Tabular View**, it is possible to click in the URI and get the XML response from the server.

Raw View, on the other hand, returns the entire response, as it would be handled by an application.

It is also possible to change the format in which the response is generated. Simply click on the drop-down **Choose** method to test from **GET(application/xml)** to **GET(application/json)** and click **Test**. Then click on **Raw View** to get a glimpse of the response.

Creating a web service client

In this recipe, we will use Google Maps to show how NetBeans enables developers to quickly create an application using web services provided by third parties.

Getting ready

It is required to have NetBeans with Java EE support installed to continue with this recipe.

If this particular NetBeans version is not available in your machine, please visit:

`http://netbeans.org`

We will use the GlassFish Server in this recipe, since it is the only server that supports Java EE 6 at the moment.

For our recipe to work, we will need a valid key for the Google Maps API. The key can be found at:

`http://code.google.com/apis/maps/signup.html`

On the site, we will generate the key. Tick the box that says **I have read and agree with the terms and conditions**, after reading and agreeing of course.

Under **My website URL**, enter:

`http://localhost:8080`

Or the correct port in which GlassFish is registered.

Then click on **Generate API key**.

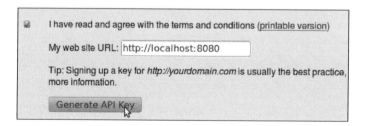

The generated key looks something like:

```
ABQIAFDAc4cEkV3R2yqZ_ooaRGXD1RT8M0brOpm-All5BF9Po1KBxRWWERQsusT9yyKEXQ
AGcYfTLTyArx88Uw
```

Save this key, we will be using it later.

How to do it...

Creating the Java Web Project

1. Click **File** and then **New Project** or Press *Ctrl+Shift+N*.

2. For **New Project**: On the **Categories** side, choose **Java Web** and on the **Projects side**, select **WebApplication**.

3. Click **Next**.

4. For **Name and Location**, under Project Name, enter **WebServiceClient**.

5. Tick the box on **Use Dedicated Folder for Storing Libraries**.

6. Now, either type the folder path or select one by clicking on **browse**.

7. After choosing the folder, we can proceed by clicking **Next**.

8. For **Server and Settings**: Under **Server**, choose **GlassFish Server 3.1**.

9. Leave the other options with their default values and click **Finish**.

Creating Servlet

Right-click on the **WebServiceClient** project, and select **New** and then **Servlet....**

1. For **New Servlet**: Under **Class Name**, enter `WSClientServlet`.

2. And under **package**, enter **servlet**.

3. Click **Finish**.

When the WSClientServlet opens in the editor, remove the code starting with:

```
/* TODO output your page here
```

And ending with:

```
*/
```

And save the file.

Adding a Web Service

Navigate to the **Services** window and expand the **Web Services** node, followed by **Google**, and finally **Map Service**.

Accepting a security certificate is required to access this service and to continue with the recipe. Please refer the following screenshot:

Drag and drop `getGoogleMap` into our Servlets `processRequest` method.

A new window, **Customize getGoogleMap SaaS Service**, pops-up.

1. Under **Input Parameters**, double-click the cell on the **address** row under the **Default Value** column, to change the value to the desired address (or keep it default if the provided one is okay).

2. Click **OK**.

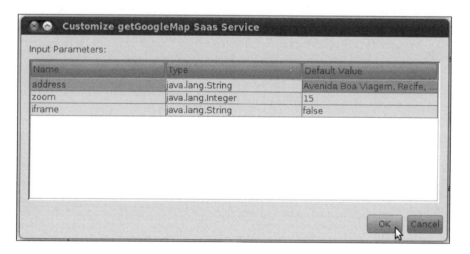

When the new block of code is written by NetBeans, uncomment the following line:

```
//out.println("The SaasService returned: "+result.getDataAsString());
```

Remember the key generated in the Getting Ready section?

In the Projects window, expand the **Source Packages** node and the package `org.netbeans.saas.google`, and double-click on `googlemapservice.properties`.

Paste the key after the **=** operator.

The line should look like:

```
api_key=ABQIAFDAc4cEkV3R2yqZ_ooaRGXD1RT8M0brOpm-All5BF9Po1KBxRWWERQsu
sT9yyKEXQAGcYfTLTyArx88Uw
```

Save file, open `WSClientServlet` and press *Shift+F6*.

When the Set Servlet Execution URI window pops-up, click **OK**.

The browser will open with our application path already in place and it will display this:

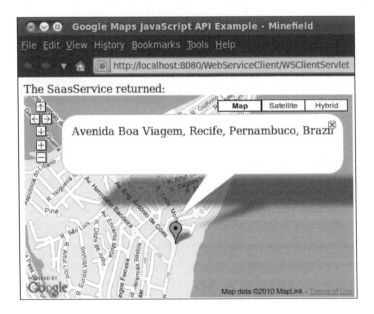

How it works...

After dragging and dropping the Google Web Service to our class, a folder structure is created by NetBeans:

Let's check what is in our folder structure:

- **GoogleMapsService.java**: Responsible for checking the coordinates given by the developer, and checks and reads the key from the properties file.

  - ❑ Returns HTML text to access GoogleMap.

- **RestConnection.java**: Responsible for establishing the connection to the Google servers.

- **RestResponse.java**: Holds the actual data returned from Google.

- **GoogleMapsService**: The class that our Servlet uses to interact with the other classes and Google.

There's more...

Discovering other web services bundled with the IDE.

Other services

There are many other web services available in the Web Service section of the IDE.

Services such as:

- Amazon: EC2 and S3
- Flickr
- WeatherBug

It is just a matter of checking the documentation of the service provider, and starting to code your own implementation. Try it out!

8
Mobile Development

In this chapter, we will cover:

- ▶ Creating CLDC/MIDP Applications
- ▶ Creating a CDC Application
- ▶ Using Visual Mobile Designer
- ▶ Beautifying your Mobile Application

Introduction

The Java Micro Edition, JME or more commonly known as J2ME, was built around the idea that it could be portable and that different devices, with different hardware configurations, could all make use of it.

For more information, please visit:

`http://download.oracle.com/javame/`

JME is divided in configurations and profiles. Configurations require devices to have a specific processing power, defined amount of available memory, certain kinds of network available, and so on. A profile complements the configurations giving a set of APIs or features that will be enabled on a particular device. Different profiles are actually the responsibility of the device manufacturers while configurations are defined in the JME.

In short, a profile complements a configuration. Profiles are more specific than configurations. Profiles specify which APIs and functionality will be available.

There are two different configurations that we will explore and build apps for in this chapter:

- ▶ **Connected Device Configuration (CDC)**: This is where a full JVM is supported. This configuration covers devices with higher capacity and processing power. For more information visit: `http://java.sun.com/products/cdc/`.

- ▶ **Connected Limited Device Configuration (CLDC)**: As the name suggests, this configuration is for lower-capacity devices. This covers mobile phones, PDAs, and other devices that have more limited memory. Instead of having a full JVM, a CLDC device has a KVM, which is a smaller, mobile-optimized subset of the JVM. For more information visit: `http://java.sun.com/products/cldc/`.

Reasons to develop with JME are as follows:

- ▶ Virtually any modern mobile phone supports MIDP/CLDC
- ▶ There are more than two billion devices out there to be developed for
- ▶ A huge market just waiting for the next killer app
- ▶ The great free IDE, NetBeans, that gives developers a very easy and powerful mobile development suite with code analyzer, top notch debug tools, and various components
- ▶ Big names in the mobile industry like Nokia, Sony Ericsson, and Samsung all support JME

Some of the big companies go even further in their involvement with JME by providing their own development toolkit for better integration and development of applications for specific phones.

And to add a cherry to the cake, entire companies are based around JME building games and other applications.

As you will notice, we are using Microsoft Windows as our operating system for this chapter. The only reason is because Sun/Oracle did not provide, at the time of writing, a working Sun Wireless Toolkit 3 for Linux.

And since we want to provide the full advantage of the development environment, we have opted for going with the Windows version.

Now let's dig in.

Creating CLDC/MIDP applications

In this recipe we will use **Mobile Information Device Profile** (**MIDP**) as the profile for our Mobile application.

MIDP is the best-known JME profile and provides core functionality that will run across many devices, giving apps more portability.

In later recipes we will also favor MIDP since the market for those applications has exploded in recent years and it is more enticing for developers to work in.

Keep in mind that MIDP applications should be written with memory consumption and processing power constraints/limitations in mind.

Getting ready

If NetBeans is not currently installed visit the download sections on:

`http://download.netbeans.org`

It is possible to find the full version of NetBeans that contains Java ME; upon installation remember to select the Java ME option.

With NetBeans ready, we can start coding.

How to do it...

1. Create a new project, this can be achieved by either clicking **File** and then **New Project** or pressing *Ctrl+Shift+N*.

2. On the **New Project** window on **Categories** side choose **Java ME** and on the **Projects** side select **Mobile Application**, then click **Next**.

3. Under **Name and Location**: Name the project as `MyMIDPApp`, leave the other options with their default values and click **Next**.

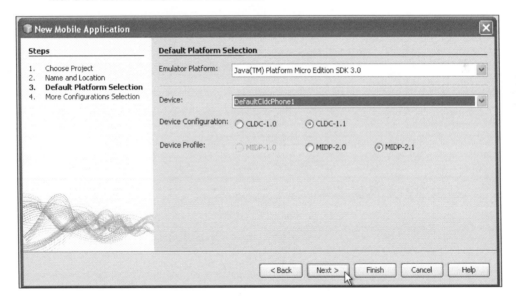

4. Under **Default Platform Selection**: On **Emulator Platform** select **Java(TM) Platform Micro Edition SDK 3.0**.

5. Click **Finish**.

How it works...

The folder structure created by NetBeans for a Java ME project is rather extensive. The project is created with an **Ant build file**, which already includes several targets. On top of that `.properties` files are created for the convenience of the developer.

To have access to all of the files shown in the screenshot below it is necessary to build the project. To do this right-click on the project and select **Build**.

After the build step, navigate to the Files window and expand the nodes to see the properties files. They each have different roles:

▶ `Projects.properties`: contains sets of key/values pairs that aid developers in configuring the project.

▶ `Genfiles.properties`: used by the IDE to track the changes generated by the build.

▶ `Private.properties`: specific to versioning and deployment of the application.

Also present is a MANIFEST file. This file is accessed by the device to show the version number and name of the application when installed in the mobile.

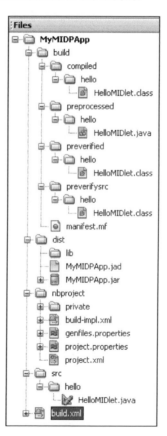

NetBeans then creates the `HelloMidlet.java`, which is our main class for developing with Java ME. For now, this is where the entire code of our project placed.

It is possible to edit the code in different ways:

- **Source View**: This is where the developer can write the code. By clicking on it the view changes to the Java Code editor, where it is possible to see the code generated by the IDE (the grayed-out and commented parts) and the user-editable content.

- **Screen View**: Allows the developer to build the UI graphically by dragging and dropping components from the Palette window.

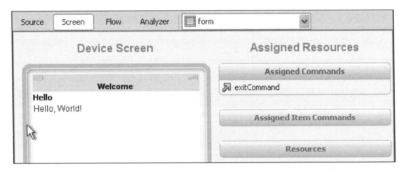

- **Flow View**: Lets the developer create and build the flow between windows and add behaviors, in the form of commands, to the components from the Palette window. This is shown in a very user-friendly and graphical way to the developer, very similar to UML diagrams.

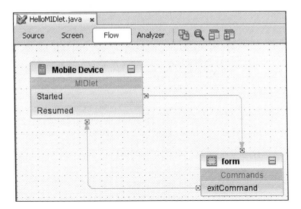

- **Analyzer View**: Since every part of memory counts in mobile applications, this view is responsible for analyzing the code for unused components, screens, or resources that might be left on our mobile application.

To run our first Mobile Application, simply right-click on our projects node and select **run**.

There's more...

There is more than one way to run your project with different devices.

Deploying applications on different device models

On project creation, we can pick the device we are designing our app for and will be deploying on.

Click on the **Default Platform Selection** dropdown and the list will be presented.

If a project already exists we can change the target device:

1. Right-click on the mobile project, in our case **MyMIDPApp**, and select **Properties**.

2. Click on **Platform** and under **Device**, it is possible to check the available phones.

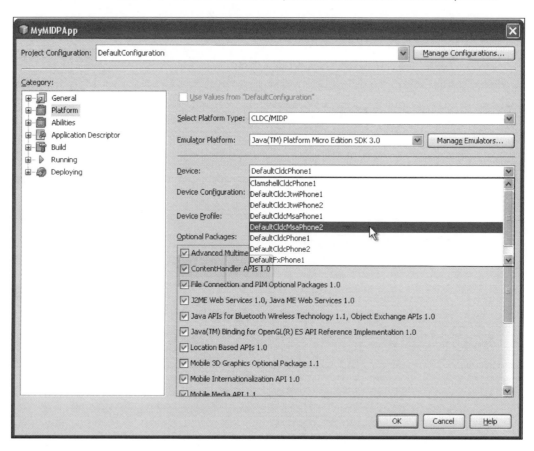

The function of the **optional packages** selected in the above screenshot is to enable features in the JME application that would otherwise be not supported. For example, the ContentHandler API lets applications execute other registered applications by URL. To learn more about this specific API visit:

```
http://download.oracle.com/javame/config/cldc/opt-pkgs/api/ch/jsr211/
index.html
```

For the other available APIs please refer to:

```
http://download.oracle.com/javame/
```

Alternatively, when testing, it is possible to select the device prior to running the application. Right-click on the project node and select **Run With**... and you will be presented with the Quick Project Run dialog:

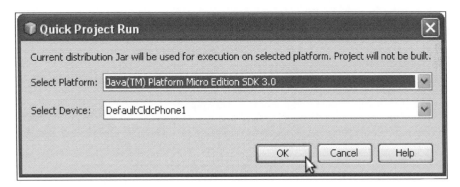

Adding more Platforms

Java comes pre-loaded in many different devices. One of the biggest deployments of Java in the mobile phone world is in Symbian phones. Symbian contains many different types, Symbian^3, S40, and so on.

We will add the SDK to work with S40 devices.

First visit:

```
http://www.forum.nokia.com/Library/Tools_and_Downloads/
```

Create an account and download the S40 fifth edition Java SDK.

Upon installation completion, go to NetBeans:

1. Click on **Tools** and **Java Platform**.

2. On the **Java Platform Manager** window, click on **Add Platform**.

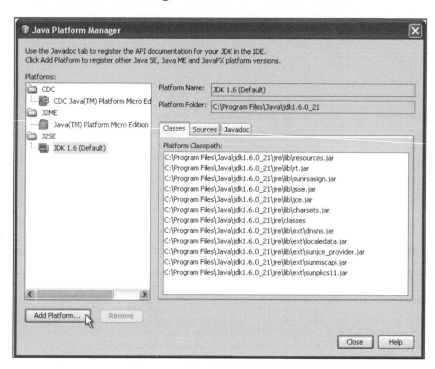

3. Under **Select Platform Type**: select **Java ME MIDP Platform Emulator** and click Next >.

4. Under **Platform Folders**: Be sure that **Nokia S40 platform** is shown and click Next >.

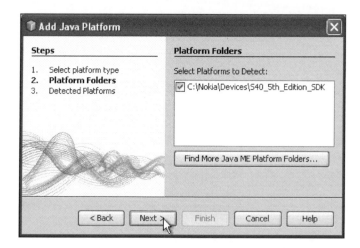

5. Under **Detected Platforms**: Select the **Nokia S40 platform SDK** and click Finish.

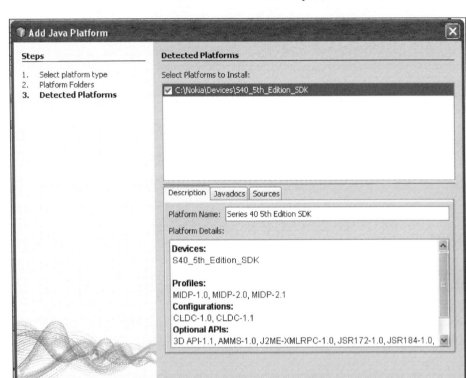

6. Back on Java Platform Manager the JME available platforms will now contain the Series 40 5th Edition SDK.

7. Click **Close**.

8. Now right-click our project and click on **Platforms** on the right-hand side of the pane.

9. Click on the **Emulator Platform** drop down and the Series 40 5th Edition Platform will be available for choosing.

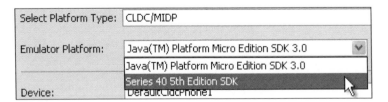

Creating CDC applications

For a CDC application we will create a project that shows the main differences between MIDP and CDC in the NetBeans context.

It is worth noting that NetBeans does in fact provide all of the components for building both configurations in a seamless manner and even changing configurations by accessing the properties of each project.

Getting ready

If NetBeans is not currently installed visit the download sections on:

`http://download.netbeans.org`

It is possible to find the full version of NetBeans, named as Java and that contains Java ME; upon installation remember to select the Java ME option.

With NetBeans ready, we can start coding.

How to do it...

1. Create a new project, this can be achieved either by clicking **File** and then **New Project** or by pressing *Ctrl+Shift+N*.

2. On the **New Project** window on the **Categories** side choose **Java ME** and on the **Projects** side select **CDC Application**, then click **Next**.

3. Under **Name and Location**: Name the project as `MyCDCApp`, leave the other options with their default values and click **Next**.

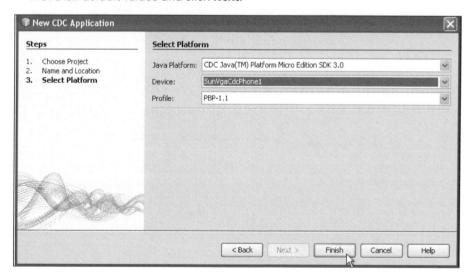

4. Under **Select Platform**: On **Emulator Platform** select **Java(TM) Platform Micro Edition SDK 3.0**.

5. Click **Finish**.

How it works...

NetBeans builds the file structure around the CDC platform. As it is common with many of the projects created by NetBeans, this project, too, is built and maintained by an Ant build file.

The project structure is rather similar to the one created for a CLDC application. One difference lies on the fact that with a CDC application we do not have the use of **Java Application Descriptor** (**JAD**) files, as evidenced when the project is built.

A JAD file is a compressed JAR file that package MIDlets. It is the JME installation file.

After being built, the file structure is as follows:

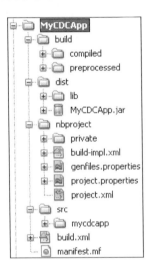

There's more...

After developing the application let's see how it goes by running the project.

Running the project

To see how the CDC project looks like in the emulator, simply right-click on our project and select **Run**.

The following screenshot shows the emulator running our project:

Using the Visual Mobile Designer

This recipe will show how the interaction between Flow and Screen view works and how to easily build an application from ground up.

Our application will consist of a splash screen, PIM browser, and login screen.

On top of that, all of the main commands and screen interaction will also be developed. We will mainly concentrate on the Flow view, Screen view, and Analyzer.

Getting ready

We will first need some image for us to show as a loading screen.

For this example we will use the Packt Publishing logo from the company web page.

Visit the page, make a screenshot out of it and save it in PNG file format with dimensions appropriate to a mobile platform. For our example we will use 127 x 68 pixels.

How to do it...

1. Create a new project, this can be achieved by either clicking **File** and then **New Project** or pressing *Ctrl+Shift+N.*

2. On the **New Project** window, on categories side choose Java ME and on the **Projects** side select **Mobile Application**, then click Next.

3. Under Name and Location : Name the project as `MyVisualMobileApp`, leave the other options with their default values, and click **Next**.

4. Under **Default Platform Selection**: On **Emulator Platform** select **Java(TM) Platform Micro Edition SDK 3.0**.

5. Under **Device** select `DefaultCldcPhone1` and click **Finish**.

On the Palette window, navigate to the **Displayables** subgroup and drag-and-drop the following components to the Flow View:

- ▶ Splash Screen
- ▶ Login Screen
- ▶ Pim Browser

All the components are shown in the following screenshot:

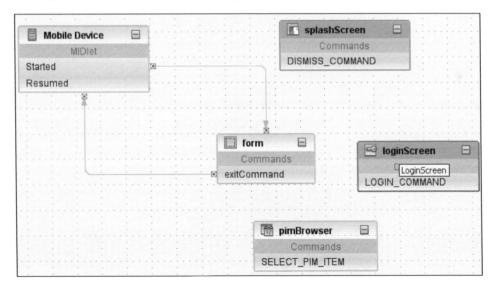

Now let's add flow and commands to the displayables. Drag the arrow that begins in the Mobile Device's Started field and ends in the form to the Splash Screen instead.

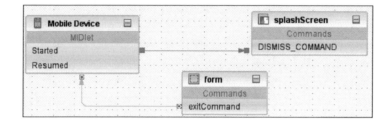

Then connect the following components:

> ▶ Connect Splash Screen to the Login Screen.

> ▶ Connect Login Screen to the PIM Browser.

To connect the screens click on the component and drag the pointer to the end component.

With the Pim Browser we will do something a bit different. We will add an **exit command** that will point to the Resumed state of the Mobile Device component. Right-click on the pimBrowser instance in the Flow View and select **New/Add** and then **Exit Command**. Then connect the newly-added exitCommand1 to the Resumed state of the Mobile Device.

The flow is shown in the following screenshot:

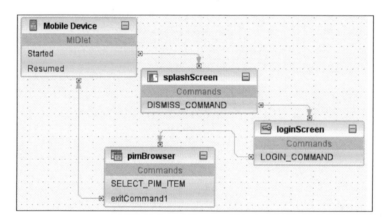

After connecting the components we will need to modify their properties. On the Flow View click on the Splash Screen and navigate to the Properties window:

1. On the Text property type **Loading**.

2. Under **Image Properties** click on the button to load the **Image Selector** window.

3. When the window pops up click on the **Add** button and **Image Path** will be available.

4. Now select an image of your choice by clicking on browse....

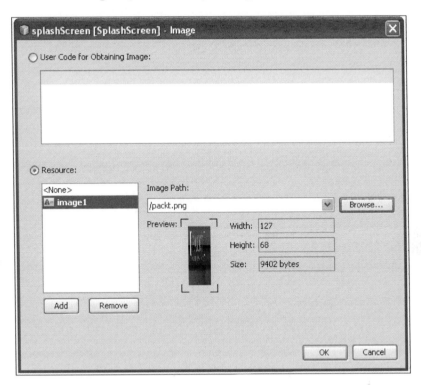

5. Click **OK** to return to the Properties window and save the file.

How it works...

NetBeans creates all the code based on our placing and linking of components. Clicking on the Source view makes it possible to check all the generated code.

All of the screen changes between Splash Screen, PIM Browser, and even exiting the MIDlet are available under the commandAction method in our file HelloMIDlet.java.

NetBeans also creates and instantiates the image file and attaches that to the splash screen together with the loading text:

```
splashScreen.setImage(getImage1());
splashScreen.setText("Loading");
```

And here is how we initialize the image:

```java
public Image getImage1() {
    if (image1 == null) {
        // write pre-init user code here
        try {
            image1 = Image.createImage("/packt.png");
        } catch (java.io.IOException e) {
            e.printStackTrace();
        }
        // write post-init user code here
    }
    return image1;
}
```

Run the project to get an idea of how the mobile application works.

There's more...

Let's see how to better organize the components in our MIDlets.

Organizing the Layout

The first button makes NetBeans re-organize the layout of the placed components. It is very useful after a lot of functionality has been added.

The Overview, the one with the magnifier, lets the developer take a broad view of all of the components, making navigation a lot easier if they become larger than one screen.

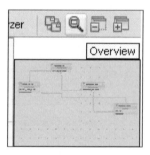

The last two buttons will collapse or expand the component boxes, hiding the command details.

Beautifying your mobile application

In this recipe we will show ways to improve the look and behavior of our mobile application.

One of the things developers will surely do when their application goes into production is brand the application with the icon of the company or development group, for a more professional look.

Getting ready

First we need to find an icon that we can use for the application.

For our application icon we can use this site to find images:

```
http://search.creativecommons.org/
```

How to do it...

Creating the project:

1. Create a new project, this can be achieved by either clicking **File** and then **New Project** or by pressing *Ctrl+Shift+N*.

2. On the **New Project** window on categories side choose Java ME and on Projects side select **Mobile Application** and click **Next**.

3. Under **Name and Location**: Name the project as `MyPrettyMobileApp`, leave the other options with their default values and click **Next**.

4. Under **Default Platform Selection**: On **Emulator Platform** select **Java(TM) Platform Micro Edition SDK 3.0**.

5. Under Device select `DefaultCldcPhone1` and click **Finish**.

Creating the images package:

1. Under the **Projects** window right-click in the **Source Package**.

2. Select **New** and click on **Java Package...**.

3. On the **New Java Package** window, name the package as **images** and click **Finish**.

4. Move all of the images that are going to be used in this package.

Now we will be adding an icon:

1. Right-click on the project and select **Properties**.

2. On the **Properties** window, click in **Libraries & Resources** and click on **Add Folder...**.

3. Navigate to the images folder and click **Open**.

4. Then navigate to **Application Descriptor** and click on the **MIDlets** tab.

5. Select our `HelloMIDlet` and click **Edit...**.

6. Clicking on the MIDlet Icon drop-down will show the image file.

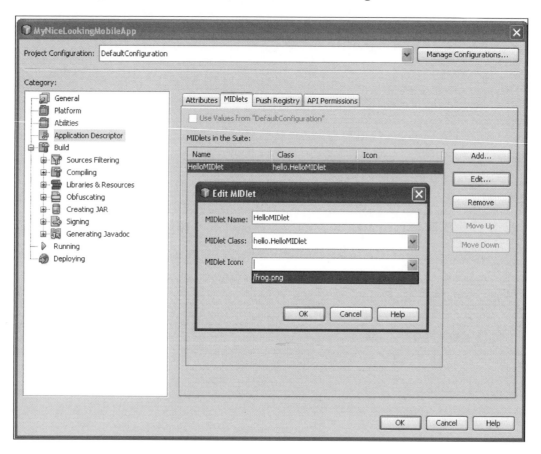

Click **OK** from the Edit MIDlet window and the IDE will refresh the icon in our `HelloMIDlet` class.

How it works...

By adding the icon to our mobile applications' **libraries & resources** we have made it possible for the image to be accessed by our code and IDE.

The **Resources** folder will show the available folder and contents when returning to the main window of the IDE.

The `project.properties` file is updated with the information containing the image:

```
manifest.midlets=MIDlet-1: HelloMIDlet,/frog.png,hello.HelloMIDlet\n
```

The image is shown when the MIDlet is run, and by exiting our application the listed MIDlet with the image is shown.

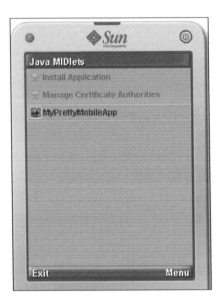

9
Java Refactoring

In this chapter, we will cover:

- ▶ Renaming elements
- ▶ Moving elements
- ▶ Extracting a superclass
- ▶ Extracting an interface
- ▶ Encapsulating fields

Introduction

NetBeans includes a comprehensive set of features for automated refactoring, that will prove very useful to developers.

In this chapter we will create examples that use NetBeans to move, extract, and create classes, methods, and interfaces.

Be warned that many of the refactoring techniques presented in this chapter might break some code. NetBeans, and other IDEs for that matter too, make it easier to revert changes but of course be wary of things going wrong.

With that in mind, let's dig in.

Renaming elements

This recipe focuses on how the IDE handles the renaming of all elements of a project, being the project itself, classes, methods, variables, and packages.

How to do it...

Let's create the code to be renamed:

1. Create a new project, this can be achieved by either clicking **File** and then **New Project** or pressing *Ctrl+Shift+N*.

2. On **New Project** window, choose **Java** on the **Categories** side, and on the **Projects** side select **Java Application**. Then click **Next**.

3. Under **Name and Location** : name the project as **RenameElements** and click **Finish**.

With the project created we will need to clear the `RenameElements.java` class of the main method and insert the following code:

```java
package  renameelements;
import java.io.File;
public class RenameElements {
    private void printFiles(String string) {
        File file = new File(string);
        if (file.isFile()) {
            System.out.println(file.getPath());
        } else if (file.isDirectory()) {
            for(String directory : file.list())
                printFiles(string + file.separator + directory);
        }
        if (!file.exists())
            System.out.println(string + " does not exist.");
    }
}
```

The next step is to rename the package, so place the cursor on top of the package name, **renameelements**, and press *Ctrl+R*.

A **Rename** dialog pops-up with the package name. Type **util** under **New Name** and click on **Refactor**.

Our class contains several variables we can rename:

1. Place the cursor on the top of the String parameter named **string** and press *Ctrl+R*.
2. Type **path** and press *Enter*.

Let's rename the other variables:

1. Rename **file** into **filePath**.

To rename methods, perform the steps below:

1. Place the cursor on the top of the method declaration, **printFiles**, right-click it then select **Refactor** and **Rename...**.
2. On the **Rename Method** dialog, under **New Name** enter **recursiveFilePrinting** and press **Refactor**.

Then let's rename classes:

1. To rename a class navigate to the **Projects** window and press *Ctrl+R* on the RenameElements.java file.
2. On the **Rename Class** dialog enter **FileManipulator** and press **Enter**.

And finally renaming an entire project:

1. Navigate to the **Project** window, right-click on the project name, **RenamingElements**, and choose **Rename...**.

2. Under **Project Name** enter **FileSystem** and tick **Also Rename Project Folder**; after that, click on **Rename**.

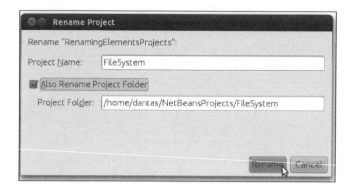

How it works...

Renaming a project works a bit differently from renaming a variable, since in this action NetBeans needs to rename the folder where the project is placed. The *Ctrl+R* shortcut is not enough in itself so NetBeans shows the Rename Project dialog. This emphasizes to the developer that something deeper is happening.

When renaming a project, NetBeans gives the developer the possibility of renaming the folder where the project is contained to the same name of the project. This is a good practice and, more often than not, is followed.

Moving elements

NetBeans enables the developer to easily move classes around different projects and packages.

No more breaking compatibility when moving those classes around, since all are seamlessly handled by the IDE.

Getting ready

For this recipe we will need a Java project and a Java class so we can exemplify how moving elements really work.

The exisiting code, created in the previous recipe, is going to be enough. Also you can try doing this with your own code since moving classes are not such a complicated step that can't be undone.

Let's create a project:

1. Create a new project, which can be achieved either by clicking **File** and then **New Project** or pressing *Ctrl+Shift+N*.

2. In the **New Project** window, choose **Java** on the **Categories** side and **Java Application** on the **Projects** side, then click **Next**.

3. Under **Name and Location**, name the Project as MovingElements and click **Finish**.

4. Now right-click on the **movingelements** package, select **New...** and **Java Class...**.

5. On the **New Java Class** dialog enter the class name as **Person**.

6. Leave all the other fields with their default values and click **Finish**.

How to do it...

1. Place the cursor inside of `Person.java` and press *Ctrl+M*.

2. Select a working project from **Project** field.

3. Select **Source Packages** in the **Location** field.

4. Under the To Package field enter: classextraction:

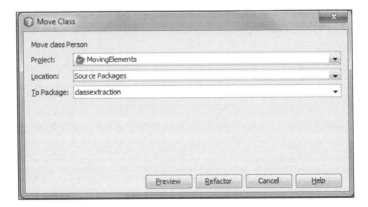

How it works...

When clicking the **Refactor** button the class is removed from the current project and placed in the project that was selected from the dialog.

The package in that class is then updated to match.

Extracting a superclass

Extracting superclasses enables NetBeans to add different levels of hierarchy even after the code is written.

Usually, requirements changing in the middle of development, and rewriting classes to support inheritance would quite complicated and time-consuming.

NetBeans enables the developer to create those superclasses in a few clicks and, by understanding how this mechanism works, even creates superclasses that extend other superclasses.

Getting ready

We will need to create a Project based on the *Getting Ready* section of the previous recipe, since it is very similar.

The only change from the previous recipe is that this recipe's project name will be **SuperClassExtraction**.

After project creation:

1. Right-click on the **superclassextraction** package, select **New...** and **Java Class...**.
2. On the **New Java Class** dialog enter the class name as **DataAnalyzer**.
3. Leave all the other fields with their default values and click **Finish**.

Replace the entire content of the DataAnalyzer.java with the following code:

```java
package superclassextraction;

import java.util.ArrayList;

public class DataAnalyzer {
    ArrayList<String> data;
    static final boolean CORRECT = true;
    static final boolean INCORRECT = false;

    private void fetchData() {
        //code
    }

    void saveData() {
    }

    public boolean parseData() {
```

```
            return CORRECT;
    }

    public String analyzeData(ArrayList<String> data, int offset) {
        //code
        return "";
    }
}
```

Now let's extract our superclass.

How to do it...

1. Right-click inside of the `DataAnalyzer.java` class, select **Refactor** and **Extract Superclass....**

2. When the **Extract Superclass** dialog appears, enter **Superclass Name** as **Analyzer.**

3. On **Members to Extract**, **select all members**, but leave **saveData** out.

4. Under the **Make Abstract** column select **analyzeData()** and leave **parseData(), saveData(), fetchData()** out. Then click **Refactor.**

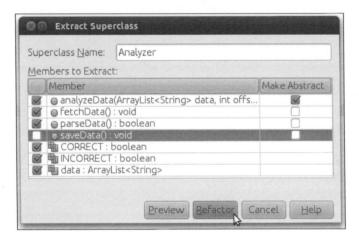

How it works...

When the **Refactor** button is pressed, NetBeans copies the marked methods from `DataAnalyzer.java` and re-creates them in the superclass.

NetBeans deals intelligently with methods marked as abstract. The abstract methods are moved up in the hierarchy and the implementation is left in the concrete class. In our example analyzeData is moved to the abstract class but marked as abstract; the real implementation is then left in DataAnalyzer.

NetBeans also supports the moving of fields, in our case the CORRECT and INCORRECT fields.

The following is the code in `DataAnalyzer.java`:

```java
public class DataAnalyzer extends Analyzer {
    public void saveData() {
        //code
    }

    public String analyzeData(ArrayList<String> data, int offset) {
        //code
        return "";
    }
}
```

The following is the code in `Analyzer.java`:

```java
public abstract class Analyzer {
    static final boolean CORRECT = true;
    static final boolean INCORRECT = false;
    ArrayList<String> data;

    public Analyzer() {
    }

    public abstract String analyzeData(ArrayList<String> data, int
    offset);

    public void fetchData() {
        //code
    }

    public boolean parseData() {
    //code
        return DataAnalyzer.CORRECT;
    }
}
```

There's more...

Let's learn how to implement parent class methods.

Implementing parent class methods

Let's add a method to the parent class:

1. Open `Analyzer.java` and enter the following code:

    ```
    public void clearData(){
        data.clear();
    }
    ```

2. Save the file.

3. Open `DataAnalyzer.java`, press *Alt+Insert* and select **Override Method...**.

4. In the **Generate Override Methods** dialog select the **clearData()** option and click **Generate**.

5. NetBeans will then override the method and add the implementation to `DataAnalyzer.java`:

    ```
    @Override
    public void clearData() {
        super.clearData();
    }
    ```

Extracting an interface

As with *Extracting a superclass*, NetBeans also enables the developer to create interfaces out of pre-existing concrete classes.

As with superclasses, it is also possible to create a more complex hierarchy when extending different interfaces and combining them together.

Getting ready

We will need to create a project based on the *Getting Ready* section of the previous recipe, since it is very similar.

The only change from the previous recipe is that this recipe's project name will be **InterfaceExtraction**.

1. Now right-click on the interfaceextraction package, select **New...** and **Java Class...**.

2. On the **New Java Class** dialog enter the class **Name** as **DataAnalyzer**.

3. Leave all the other fields with their default values and click **Finish**.

Replace the entire content of `DataAnalyzer.java` with the following code:

```java
package interfaceextraction;

import java.util.ArrayList;

public class DataAnalyzer {
    ArrayList<String> data;
    static final boolean CORRECT = true;
    static final boolean INCORRECT = false;

    private void fetchData() {
        //code
    }

    void saveData() {
    }

    public boolean parseData() {
        return CORRECT;
    }

    public String analyzeData(ArrayList<String> data, int offset) {
        //code
        return "";
    }
}
```

Now let's extract our interface.

How to do it...

1. Right-click inside of the **DataAnalyzer.java** class, select **Refactor** and **Extract Interface...**.

2. When the **Extract Interface** dialog appears, enter **Interface Name** as **IDataAnalyzer**.

3. On **Members to Extract** select both methods and click **Refactor**.

How it works...

NetBeans copies the method declaration of selected methods contained in our concrete class and creates an interface with them.

Then our concrete class is marked with the **implements** keyword.

The interface is then placed in the same package as our concrete class.

```
package interfaceextraction;
import java.util.ArrayList;
public interface IDataAnalyzer {
    String analyzeData(ArrayList<String> data, int offset);
    boolean parseData();
}
```

There's more...

Extracting interface from classes that already have an interface; undoing interface extraction; and understanding the options when refactoring.

Creating interfaces for classes that already implement interfaces

Let's create another interface directly from the class that already implements an interface.

Change the access modifier of fetchData method from default to public:

```
public void saveData() {
    //code
}
```

Perform the Extract Interface process one more time:

1. Right-click inside of the **DataAnalyzer.java** class, select **Refactor** and **Extract Interface...**.

2. When the **Extract Interface** dialog appears, enter as **Interface Name** **IDatabaseAccess**.

3. On **Members to Extract**, this time select implements **IDataAnalyzer** and **saveData** and click **Refactor**.

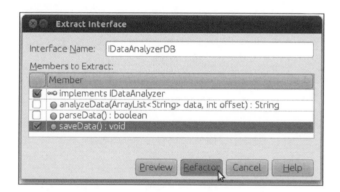

As seen in the previous screenshot another option is given to the developer, the **implements IDataAnalzyer**.

This option will replace the interface that the class is currently implementing with the newly generated one, and then extend that new interface with the original.

Here is some code to exemplify:

Our class:

```
public class DataAnalyzer implements IDataAnalyzerDB
```

Our new interface:

```
public interface IDataAnalyzerDB extends IDataAnalyzer
```

Undoing interface exctraction

Don't worry, NetBeans is well-prepared for this situation.

Simply right-click `DataAnalyzer.java`, and inside of the **Refactor** sub-menu there is the **Undo [Extract Interface]** option.

Refactoring options

When clicking Preview in the Extracting Interface the developer is presented with the Refactoring Options.

In this window it is possible to go into great detail over what will get refactored during the above tasks.

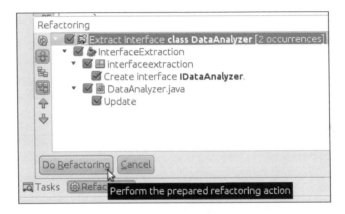

In this dialog we can select any, all or none of the hierarchical options.

It is possible, for example, not to enable the creation of the interface, even though this would have the consequence of code not compiling, but this gives the developer the chance to make necessary changes to whatever is needed.

Encapsulating fields

Encapsulation is one of the core principles of object-oriented programming and NetBeans goes to great lengths to simplify the process of generating the necessary code for it.

Getting ready

Creating the code to be encapsulated:

We will need to create a project based on the first *Getting Ready* section of this chapter, since it is very similar.

The only change from the previous recipe is that this recipe's project name will be **EncapsulatingFieldsProject**.

We will also need to add a Java class with **Person** as the class name with **entities** as the package name.

Replace the code within `Person.java` with:

```java
package entities;

public class Person {
    long id;
    String firstName;
    String lastName;
    int age;
    String address;
    String email;
}
```

And save the file.

How to do it...

With `Person.java` open in the Java editor:

1. Right-click inside of `Person.java`.

2. Select **Refactor** and **Encapsulate Fields...**.

3. On the **Encapsulate Fields** dialog, in the top right corner click on **Select All** and then click **Refactor**.

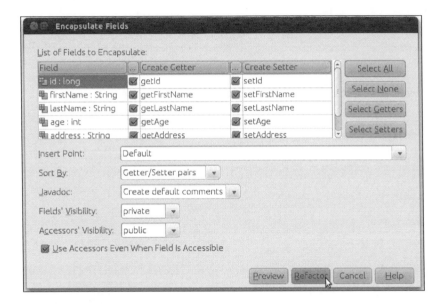

How it works...

NetBeans does a great job when creating all the getters and setters with the default values, even letting the developer select each individual method for each property.

This gives a good balance of what should be made accessible and how it should be accessible.

By leaving all of the default options in the field, NetBeans marks all variables as private, adds get/set methods for each variable and documents them.

Here is a snippet of the generated code for the firstName property:

```
private String firstName;
    /**
     * @return the firstName
     */
    public String getFirstName() {
        return firstName;
    }
```

```
/**
 * @param firstName the firstName to set
 */
public void setFirstName(String firstName) {
    this.firstName = firstName;
}
```

There's more...

We will better understand the many options provided by the Encapsulate dialog in NetBeans by considering what follows.

Understanding encapsulate fields options

The options presented by the **Encapsulate Field** dialog are very straightforward:

- **Sort By** NetBeans will sort the access methods depending on the option selected.
- **Getter/Setter** pair organizes the methods by their common field.
- **Getter then Setters** organizes the methods with all the getters preceding setters.
- **Method Name** organizes methods by their own names.

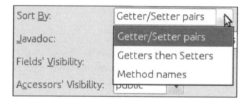

Javadoc option enforces the location where the Javadoc for the accessor methods will come from.

Be it by copying from the fields with the **Copy from field** option, letting the IDE do the hard work of creating the Javadoc for all of the methods with **Create default comments**, or simply **None**.

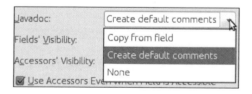

Field Visibility enables the developer to choose which Java access modifier should be applied to the variable declaration:

Accessor Visibility enables the developer to choose which Java access modifier should be applied to the accessor methods (get/set).

10
Extending the IDE

In this chapter, we will cover:

- ▶ Creating a new Project Wizard
- ▶ Creating a new File Wizard
- ▶ Creating Options Panel

Introduction

NetBeans runs on the NetBeans Platform. A vast array of developed components and actions greatly reduces the amount of effort developers need when building desktop applications (such as NetBeans itself) or developing any plugins that would be associated with it.

If you wish to learn more about the NetBeans Platform, go to:

```
http://netbeans.org/features/platform/
```

And for a more detailed look at the platform documentation:

```
http://netbeans.org/features/platform/all-docs.html
```

In this chapter we will create our own plugins that will be integrated into the IDE itself.

There are a number of reasons for doing this, such as contributing to the NetBeans project, developing plugins for your own purposes or even re-branding the IDE to suit your company needs.

Creating a new project Wizard

A wizard is a step-by-step assistant that helps the user to enter information in a structured manner.

NetBeans offers the developer the option to create a wide variety of wizards. These wizards can be non-sequential in nature, further enhancing the user experience.

Getting ready

To create a NetBeans Module follow the steps below:

1. Create a new project, this can be achieved by either clicking **File** and then **New Project** or pressing *Ctrl+Shift+N*.

2. On **New Project** window on Categories side select **NetBeans Modules** and on **Projects side** select **Module** and click **Next >**.

3. Under **Name and Location**, Under **Project Name** enter NBCookbookWizard and leave all the default values as they are and click **Next >**.

4. Under **Basic Module Configuration**, Under **Code Name** Base enter com.packtpub.

5. Then select **Generate XML Layer**, leave the default value and click **Finish**.

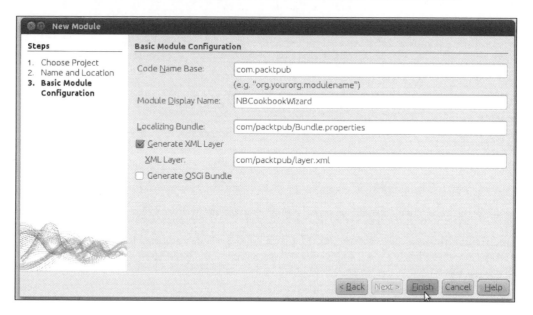

How to do it...

Now with the project created, perform the following steps to create the wizard:

1. Right-click project node, select **New** then **Other...**.

2. On **New File** window on **Categories** side choose **Module Development** and on the **File Types** side select **Wizard** and click **Next >**.

3. On **New Wizard** dialog, **Wizard Type**: Leave **Registration type** with its own default value (**Custom**).

4. Leave with the default value **Wizard Type Sequence** (**Static**).

5. Under **Number of Wizard Panels** enter **3** and click **Next**.

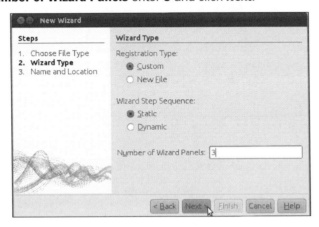

6. Under **Name and Location**: Under enter first under Class Name Prefix and let NetBeans fill the other details. Then click **Finish**.

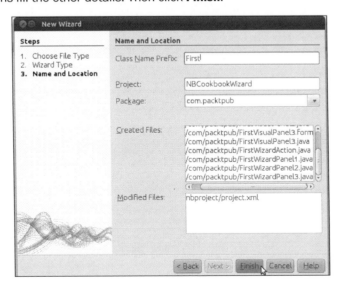

Now let's modify `FirstWizardAction.java`, replacing the following line:

```
wizardDescriptor.setTitle("Your wizard dialog title here");
```

with this:

```
wizardDescriptor.setTitle("Project Wizard");
```

Then save the file.

Now to add components to our panel. Open `FirstVisualPanel1.java` and add the following Swing components:

- ▶ 2 Labels
- ▶ 2 TextFields

1. Replace the default text of the first Label (can be done by double-clicking on it) and write **Name**.
2. Replace the text of the second Label with **Location**.
3. Then right-click on the other two TextFields, select **Edit Text** in each one of them and delete the attached text.
4. Now click on the **Source** button and on the `getName()` method replace the String **Step #1** with **Name and Location**.
5. Save the file.

Open `FirstVisualPane2.java` and add the following Swing components:

- ▶ 2 Labels
- ▶ 2 RadioButtons
- ▶ 1 TextArea

Replace the default text of the first Label with **Description**, and the text of the second Label with **Type**.

Click on the first RadioButton and on the **Properties** window (on the right side of the IDE) under the **Other Properties** sub-section replace the text in the Label property with **Web**.

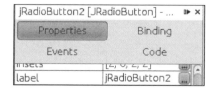

Do the same thing to the second RadioButton, but this time under **Label** enter **Desktop**.

Now click on the **Source** button and on the `getName()` method replace the String **Step #2** with **Project Description**, then the file. And finally the last FirstVisualPane. Open `FirstVisualPane3.java` and add the following Swing components:

- ▶ 2 Labels
- ▶ 1 ComboBox
- ▶ 1 TextArea

1. Replace the default text of the first Label with **Server**.
2. Replace the text of the second Label with **Environment**.
3. For the ComboBox click on the **Properties** window, then under the Properties sub-section click on the **find the model** property.

On the right-hand side of the property there is a button with three dots (...) that will let the developer replace the text with the following:

- ▶ Oracle GlassFish Server
- ▶ Apache Tomcat
- ▶ JBoss

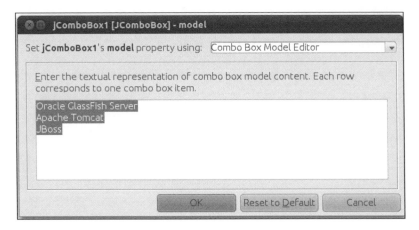

Now click on the **Source** button and on the `getName()` method replace the String **Step #3** with **Servers**. Click **OK** and save the file.

Open `layer.xml` and replace the following code:

```
<filesystem/>
```

with

```
<filesystem>
    <folder name="Toolbars">
        <folder name="File">
```

```
            <file name="com-packtpub-FirstWizardAction.shadow">
                <attr name="originalFile" stringvalue="Actions/File/
com-packtpub-FirstWizardAction.instance"/>
            </file>
        </folder>
    </folder>
    <folder name="Actions">
        <folder name="File">
            <file name="com-packtpub-FirstWizardAction.instance">
                <attr name="delegate" newvalue="com.packtpub.
FirstWizardAction"/>
                <attr name="instanceCreate" methodvalue="org.openide.
awt.Actions.alwaysEnabled"/>
            </file>
        </folder>
    </folder>
</filesystem>
```

Save the file and click on **Run**.

How it works...

When **Generate XML Layer** is selected NetBeans creates the `layer.xml` file in the specified directory (which can be changed depending on preference).

The `layer.xml` file registers our component to NetBeans, in our case a new wizard will be added to the toolbar.

On the **New Wizard** dialog on the **Wizard** type step we have selected **Registration Type** as **Custom** so that the user will have a sequential progress in each wizard step.

Selecting **Custom** as **Wizard Type** also has an effect on which files NetBeans will create for arranging the wizard.

The files created by NetBeans for the wizard are:

▶ `FirstWizardAction.java`: responsible for registration and behavior of the component as a whole.

▶ `FirstVisualPanelX.java`: one created for each of the panels. X can be replaced by the number of selected panels. It is where the wizard is designed and other components, like labels and textfields are placed.

▶ `FirstWizardPanelX.java`: as with `FirstVisualPanel.java`, one is created for each panel. This is where data that was entered in the Visual Panels is then retrieved and stored so that it can be available to the wizard action.

This is also an easier and faster way to create wizards other than fiddling around with combinations of **Registration Types** and **Wizard Step Sequence**.

For the Wizard Step Sequence option we went for keeping things simple and selecting the **Static** option. This prevents the wizard user this will prevent it from "jumping" between wizard panels giving a more linear progress which might give a more restrictive experience. For the developer it means easier way to implement it, since the developer wont need to keep track of all possible combinations.

After saving and running the files the results should look like this: `FirstVisualPanel1.java`.

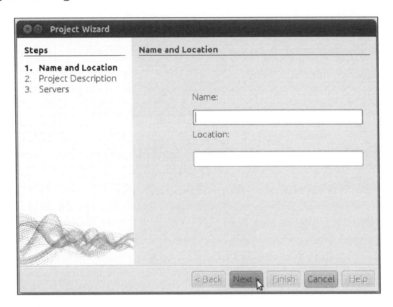

There's more...

Implementing another kind of wizard. Also, how to add your own icon to the toolbar.

Different wizard behavior

There are other ways the wizard can be created that will result in different interactions with the user and vary the amount of work/flexibility involved.

On the second step of the **New Wizard** dialog, the **Wizard** type, choose **Registration Type** as **Custom** and **Wizard Step Sequence** as **Dynamic**.

This new wizard will provide the functionality of jumping between panels. This will provide more flexibility to the user but with the added expense to the developer that will be forced to handle the non-linear progression between panels.

The file list is almost the same as the one we have seen in the recipe example. The difference being that now we will have the `WizardIterator.java`, which is created to handle these panel changes.

The file list is also almost identical to the previous examples but with the notable addition of an HTML file which is responsible for holding the description of the wizard itself.

As with the previous example, the WizardIterator is responsible for providing the directions that the wizard will take.

Adding an icon

Notice that when running our example there is no default icon for the placeholder of our new wizard. NetBeans uses a missing icon image as the default one.

To add an icon follow the steps below:

1. Open `layer.xml`.

2. Find the following line:

   ```
   <file name="com-packtpub-FirstWizardAction.instance">
   ```

3. Right before the `</file>` tag add (Supposing our image is named as `picon.png`):

   ```
   <attr name="iconBase" stringvalue="com/packtpub/picon.png"/>
   ```

4. Now add the image to the directory where all the Java sources are placed, in our case the `src/com/packtpub`.

5. Save and re-run the example. The Wizard with the new image is placed near the **File** menu toolbar.

Creating a new file wizard

The **new file wizard** works similarly as the previous chapter wizard function with the difference that this works, as the name suggests, by allocating a placeholder for a desired file type, say a Python source file.

Another difference from the previous wizard is that in this one we will use FreeMarker, a template engine to generate text. By creating the FreeMarker templates the developer can then combine the templates with data, generating text of pages as a result.

For more information visit: `http://freemarker.org`.

Getting ready

We will need to create a New Project based on the **NetBeans Module**. Follow the
Getting Ready section of the previous recipe and when Project Name is asked enter
`NBCookbookFileTemplates`, using the other values as shown in the *Getting Ready* section.

How to do it...

Our recipe starts by creating a template. Right-click on the projects node, select **New**
and **Other...**.

1. Under **Choose File Type**: On the **Categories** side select **Other** and under **File Types**
   select **Empty File** and click **Next >**.

2. Under **Name and Location**: Under **File Name** enter `pythonTemplate.py`.

3. The **Folder** field click on the **Browse...** button.

4. Then on the **Browse Folders** window expand the `NBCookbookFileTemplates` until
   reaching the `com.packtpub` package and click **Select Folder**.

5. Back on the **New Empty File** dialog click **Finish**.

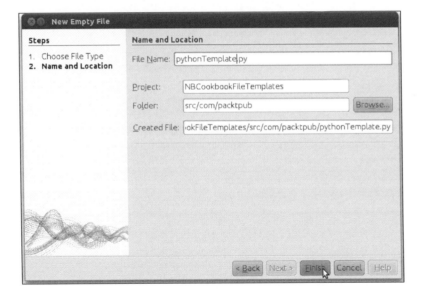

When the empty file is opened insert the following:

```
"""On ${date} at ${time} the ${nameAndExt} was created by ${user}"""
class ${name}:
    """TODO: Remove comment"""
```

Now we will need a descriptor. Right-click on the projects node, select **New** and **Other....**

1. Under **Choose File Type**: On the Categories side select **Other** and under **File Types** select **HTML File** and click **Next >**.

2. Under **Name and Location**: Under **File Name** enter: `descriptor`.

3. On the **Folder** field click on the **Browse...** button.

4. On the **Browse Folders** window expand the `NBCookbookFileTemplates` until reaching the `com.packtpub` package and click **Select Folder**.

5. Back on the **New HTML File** dialog click **Finish**.

When the HTML file is opened, in between the `<body>` tags, insert the following:

```
Python Template
```

Finally we will tie the components together by editing `layer.xml`. Replace the following tag:

```
<filesystem/>
```

with:

```
<filesystem>
<folder name="Templates">
<folder name="Other">
    <file name="Python.py" url="pythonTemplate.py">
        <attr name="template" boolvalue="true"/>
        <attr name="SystemFileSystem.localizingBundle"
stringvalue="com.packtpub.Bundle"/>
        <attr name="templateWizardURL" urlvalue="nbresloc:/com/
packtpub/descriptor.html"/>
        <attr name="javax.script.ScriptEngine"
stringvalue="freemarker"/>
    </file>
</folder>
</folder>
</filesystem>
```

Now is the turn to edit the `Bundle.properties`:

1. Expand **Source Packages** and `com.packtpub` package.

2. Double-click on `Bundle.properties` and append the following line:

   ```
   Templates/Other/Python.py=Modified Python Template
   ```

Save the file.

How it works...

The template file we have created is similar to the normal Java file template that NetBeans creates every time we ask for a new Java class.

This time we have decided to create a Python Template. The File is annotated with the following tags:

- `${date}`
- `${time}`
- `${nameAndExt}`
- `${user}`
- `${name}`

The names of the tags and their meanings are self-explanatory.

Following the creation of the Python template the descriptor is the next step. This is the information that is going to be shown to the user when clicking a file on the **New File** dialog. This file is HTML-formatted and we have just included a brief description of what our file is going to be. Note that formatting styles, such as bold and italics, might be applied with the HTML tags to give the description field a better visualization.

`layer.xml` is the file where we actually bind the code and all of the created resources together.

The `<folder>` tag indicates to the IDE where the placing of our Python template is going to be located. Both tags then indicate that this is under `Templates` and `Other`.

As said in the beginning of the recipe, FreeMarker is used as an engine for text output. The tag:

```
<attr name="javax.script.ScriptEngine" stringvalue="freemarker"/>
```

Specifies which script engine is used for that purpose.

And:

```
<attr name="SystemFileSystem.localizingBundle" stringvalue="com.
packtpub.Bundle"/>
```

Shows the IDE where the bundle file, which contains the String that is used for the name on the left side of the New File Wizard, is located.

To finally create our own Python file:

1. Run the main project.
2. When the new NetBeans instance is running create a new project.

3. When the project is created right-click on the **Project** node and select **New** and **Other....**

4. On the **New File** dialog select under **Categories** navigate to **Other** and on the **File Types** side select **Modified Python Templates**.

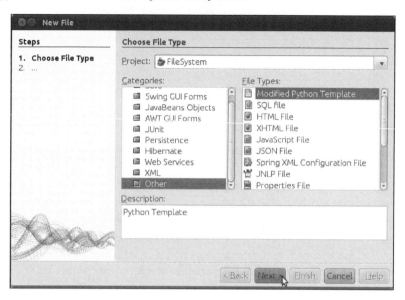

After following the wizard steps the file created has the following output:

```
"""On Dec 07, 2010 at 10:47:12 PM the testepython.py was created by
dantas"""
class testepython:
    """TODO: Remove comment"""
```

Creating options panels

More often than not, when creating plugins that will enhance an IDE the developers decide to place the configuration panels in the IDE's own options panel.

In this recipe we will learn how to create panels that will be placed together with NetBeans own options panel, but in a separate container, and also include our own options together with NetBeans, meaning that one tab will be included with NetBeans options.

Getting ready

We will need to create a new project based on **NetBeans Module**. Follow the *Getting Ready* section of the previous recipe and when **Project Name** is asked enter NBCookbookOptionsPanel, using the other values as shown in the recipe.

How to do it...

First we need to create a Options Panel.

Right-click project node, select **New** and **Other...**:

1. On **New File** dialog, choose **File Type**, under **Categories** select **Module Development** and under **File Types** select **Options Panel** and click **Next >**.

2. Under **Choose Panel Type**: Click on **Create Primary Panel**.

3. Under **Category Label** enter **PacktPub**.

4. Under **Icon (32x32)** click on **Browse...** and select a desired image (for this recipe the PacktPub logo will be used).

5. Under **Keywords** enter **Packt Pub Primary Panel** and click **Next >**.

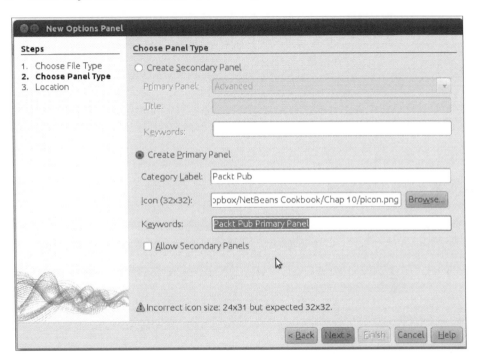

6. And finally under **Location**: Leave all fields with the default values and click **Finish**.

When NetBeans opens both `PacktPubPanel.java` and `PacktPubOptionsPanelController.java`, select `PacktPubPanel.java` in the editor and drag the following components from the Swing Palette to the editor:

- ▶ 3 Labels
- ▶ 2 TextFields

- ▶ 1 Button
- ▶ 4 CheckBoxes

Organize and rename the text of the components in the following order:

Save it.

How it works...

The example in this recipe can be executed by clicking on **Run the Main Project**. Once the new NetBeans instance is loaded click on the menu items **Tools** and then **Options**.

By selecting **Create Primary Panel** during creation we have indicated to NetBeans that we want a panel placed together with all other panel options that are already default by NetBeans, the other options being including our newly created panel in one of NetBeans panels.

On the top part of the **Options** dialog our **Primary Panel** entry is placed close to the **Miscellaneous** button as shown in the following screenshot:

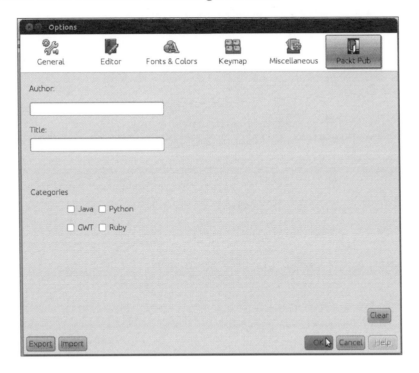

At this point our example does not load/save parameters when entered, because our panel does not have any behavior.

There's more...

How to save and load parameters, creating sub-level entries in options menu and what keywords are used for.

Saving parameters

Saving parameters is the first step to making the code in this recipe 100 percent usable.

For this we will need to open `PacktPubPanel.java` and change from Design mode to Source mode.

In Source mode, find the `store()` method and replace the comments inside of it with the following code:

```
        NbPreferences.forModule(PacktPubPanel.class).put(jLabel1.
getText().toLowerCase(), jTextField2.getText());
        NbPreferences.forModule(PacktPubPanel.class).put(jLabel2.
getText().toLowerCase(), jTextField1.getText());
        NbPreferences.forModule(PacktPubPanel.class).
putBoolean(jCheckBox1.getText().toLowerCase(), jCheckBox1.
isSelected());
        NbPreferences.forModule(PacktPubPanel.class).
putBoolean(jCheckBox2.getText().toLowerCase(), jCheckBox2.
isSelected());
        NbPreferences.forModule(PacktPubPanel.class).
putBoolean(jCheckBox3.getText().toLowerCase(), jCheckBox3.
isSelected());
        NbPreferences.forModule(PacktPubPanel.class).
putBoolean(jCheckBox4.getText().toLowerCase(), jCheckBox4.
isSelected());
```

Then save it and run the example.

The information is saved to the following file:

```
NBCookbookOptionsPanel/build/testuserdir/config/Preferences/com/
packtpub.properties
```

By opening it, it is possible to check how the data and the keys are displayed.

Loading parameters

After saving the parameters the next logical step is to load them.

This can be easily achieved by following almost the same steps as in the previous saving parameters example:

Open `PacktPubPanel.java`, find the `load()` method, and replace the comments inside of the method body with the following code:

```
        jTextField1.setText(NbPreferences.forModule(PacktPubPanel.
class).get(jLabel2.getText().toLowerCase(), ""));
        jTextField2.setText(NbPreferences.forModule(PacktPubPanel.
class).get(jLabel1.getText().toLowerCase(), ""));
        if(NbPreferences.forModule(PacktPubPanel.class).
get(jCheckBox1.getText().toLowerCase(), "").equals("true"))
            jCheckBox1.setSelected(true);
        else
            jCheckBox1.setSelected(false);
```

```
            if(NbPreferences.forModule(PacktPubPanel.class).
get(jCheckBox2.getText().toLowerCase(), "").equals("true"))
            jCheckBox2.setSelected(true);
        else
            jCheckBox2.setSelected(false);
            if(NbPreferences.forModule(PacktPubPanel.class).
get(jCheckBox3.getText().toLowerCase(), "").equals("true"))
            jCheckBox3.setSelected(true);
        else
            jCheckBox3.setSelected(false);
            if(NbPreferences.forModule(PacktPubPanel.class).
get(jCheckBox4.getText().toLowerCase(), "").equals("true"))
            jCheckBox4.setSelected(true);
        else
            jCheckBox4.setSelected(false);
```

Save the file.

Next time when the the IDE is restarted after parameters are inserted, the values will be retained.

Secondary panel

The secondary panel is the one included in NetBeans own options instead of having its own tab.

To create a secondary panel follow the following instructions:

1. Right-click project node, select **New** and **Other...**.
2. On **New File** dialog, choose **File Type**. Under Categories select **Module Development** and under **File Types** select **Options Panel** and click **Next >**.
3. Under **Panel Type**: Click on **Create Secondary Panel**.
4. On **Primary Panel** leave **Advanced** as default option.
5. Then enter **Packt Pub Secondary Panel** as **Title**.
6. And under **Keywords** enter **Packt Pub Secondary Panel** and click **Next**.
7. Under **Location**: Leave all fields with the default values and click **Finish**.

Then open the `PacktPubSecondaryPanelPanel.java` and add the following components:

▶ 2 Labels
▶ 2 TextFields

Save it and run the example by clicking on the **Run Main Project** icon.

After organizing the components and renaming them the new secondary options panel, already running in our example, should look more or less like this:

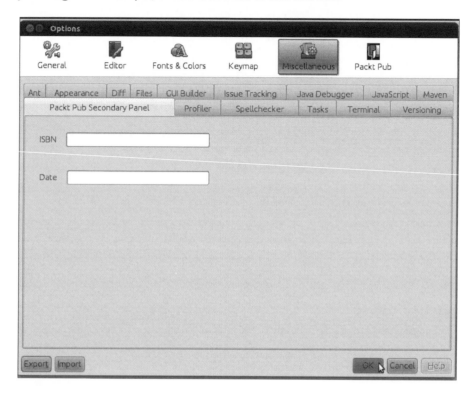

Keywords

Developer-defined keywords are used in conjunction with the quick search box.

By only typing in the quick search, for example Packt Pub, we will have the list of the matching keywords, in our case Packt Pub Primary Panel and Packt Pub Secondary Panel, as shown by the following screenshot:

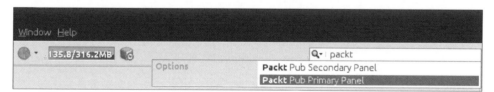

11

Profiling and Testing

In this chapter, we will cover:

- ▶ Profiling Java code
- ▶ Creating Unit Tests
- ▶ Using SQE for improved code quality
- ▶ Monitoring HTTP connections
- ▶ Using load generator (JMeter)

Introduction

This chapter is dedicated to explaining how to get the most out of NetBeans when Testing and Profiling are needed for our projects.

With NetBeans we will check how our applications are behaving in realtime. NetBeans provides graphic information on threads, memory, and CPU performance. By using the built-in profiler, developers get a very fine-grained view of possible bottlenecks in the code.

Then we will use the IDE's help to create unit tests with the JUnit framework. We will go through the process of choosing the correct JUnit version for our needs and correctly choosing the options provided by the framework.

We will also go deeper into software quality testing by using the SQE plugins, which offer functionality such as finding possible bugs, checking coding style, and identifying overly complex code.

Another section of the chapter introduces the Monitoring of HTTP Connections that helps developers to better analyze the data flow between the Application Server and their application.

Finally we will check how to integrate JMeter with NetBeans so we can test a basic web application with different kinds of stress.

All, as usual, from the comfort of your favorite IDE.

Profiling Java code

The NetBeans profiling tool gives developers the ability to inspect their developed applications while they are running. With it, it is possible to gather valuable information from the state applications are in at a determined moment.

In this recipe we will use the Profiling tool to check:

▶ Consumed CPU time

▶ Runtime behavior

▶ Memory consumption by components

The project we will use for this recipe is the Document Editor contained within the examples supplied with NetBeans. We will use the Document Editor since sources are provided together with the NetBeans installation, but feel free to apply the concepts in this recipe to your own project.

Getting ready

Since the NetBeans Profiler is already included in the installation package of the IDE there is not much difference from which version to install, but we will continue with the Java bundle provided which can be found at: `http://netbeans.org/downloads/index.html`.

First we will need to create a project:

1. Create a **New Project**, by either clicking **File** and then **New Project** or pressing *Ctrl+Shift+N*.

2. On the **New Project** window, on categories side choose **Samples** and **Java** and on Projects side select **Document Editor** and click **Next >**.

3. Under **Name and Location**: Leave all the default values and click **Finish**.

To successfully use the profiler we will have to first calibrate it. To do so, please follow the steps below:

1. On the toolbar click on **Profile**.

2. Select **Advanced Commands** and click on **Run Profiler Calibration**.

3. Select the desired **Java Platform** and click **OK**.

4. Wait for the dialog confirming successful calibration and click **OK**.

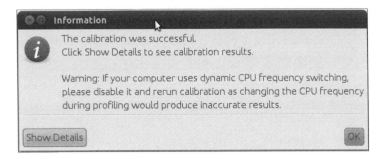

5. On the toolbar click on **Profile** and then **Profile Main Project...** (or press _Alt+F2_).

6. On the **Enable Profile of DocumentEditor** dialog press **OK**.

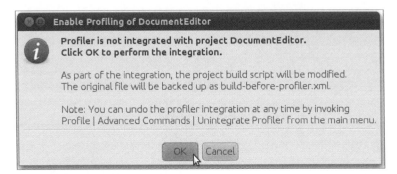

How to do it...

Let's start the profiling of our application by monitoring threads:

1. On the toolbar click on **Profile...** and then **Profile Main Project** (or press _Alt+F2_).

2. On the **Profile DocumentEditor** dialog launch, click on **Monitor**.

3. Check the **Enable threads monitoring** checkbox.

4. Click **Run**.

After monitoring the threads we will dive into profiling CPU performance.

Stop the previous profiling session (this can be done by finishing the execution of the Document Editor application) and follow the steps below:

1. On the toolbar click on **Profile...** and then **Profile Main Project** (or press *Alt+F2*).

2. On **Profile DocumentEditor** dialog launch, click on **CPU**.

3. Select **Part of Application** and click on **define**.

4. On **Specify Root Methods** click on **Add from Project...**.

5. Expand the **DocumentEditor** tree until you get to **DocumentEditorApp**, expand **Methods** and finally mark the **startup** method and click **OK**.

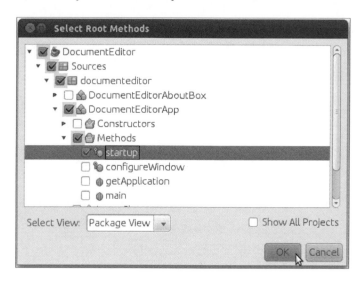

6. Back on the **Specify Root Methods** click **OK** once again and click **Run**.

The next step is to analyze how our application is consuming memory.

Stop the previous profiling session (this can be done by finishing the execution of the Document Editor application).

1. On the toolbar click on **Profile...** and then **Profile Main Project** (or press *Alt+F2*).

2. On **Profile DocumentEditor** dialog launch, click on **Memory**.

3. Select **Record** object creation only.

4. Then on the option: **Track every object allocations** enter **1** instead of **10**.

5. Select **Record stack trace for allocations**.

6. And click **Run**.

We will then proceed to the final step of saving snapshots.

With the application still running navigate to the **Profiler** window and click on **Live Results** icon.

1. Right-click inside the **Live Profiling Results** and select **Take a Snapshot** (or use *Ctrl+F2*) and show **Allocation Stack Traces**.

2. Inside of the **Memory** window, press *Ctrl+S* to save.

How it works...

Once the profiler has been integrated with the DocumentEditor, NetBeans presents the Profile DocumentEditor dialog with Monitor, CPU, and Memory options.

When starting the thread monitoring process, NetBeans will launch a window covering the place where the Java editor is.

This window will present the developer with a graph in which a timeline of threads is shown. These threads can be Running, Sleeping, Waiting, or in Monitor state.

Under the new window the developer has the possibility to change to the other views: **Table** and **Details**.

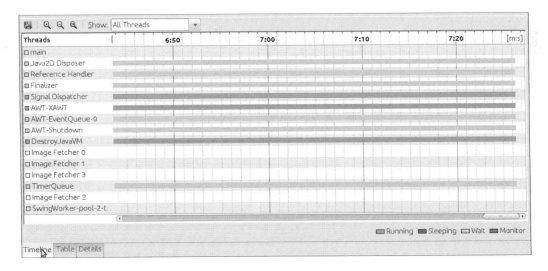

Under **Table** tab, statistics are presented which detail the Running/Sleeping/Waiting time of each thread, along with the total time of each monitoring thread.

Thread	Running ▼	Sleeping	Wait	Monitor
Signal Dispatcher	7:26.301 (100.0%)	0.0 (0.0%)	0.0 (0.0%)	0.0 (0.0%)
DestroyJavaVM	7:24.695 (100.0%)	0.0 (0.0%)	0.0 (0.0%)	0.0 (0.0%)
AWT-XAWT	7:24.495 (99.9%)	0.0 (0.0%)	0.301 (0.0%)	0.0 (0.0%)
AWT-EventQueue-0	4.861 (1.0%)	0.0 (0.0%)	7:19.834 (98.9%)	0.0 (0.0%)

The **Details** tab presents pie charts and timelines of each of the threads in the application, giving a complete visualization of both timeline and Table views, which is useful for identifying bottlenecks in the application.

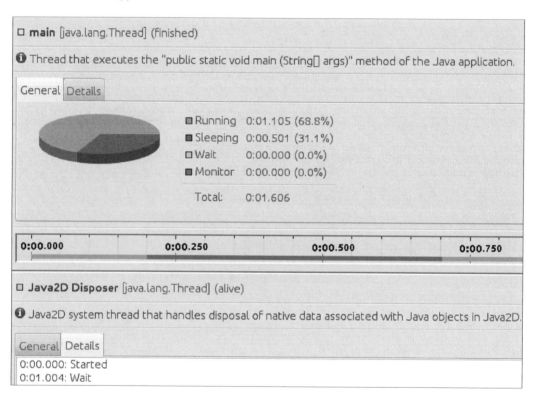

It is possible to click on each of the colors in the timeline and navigate to the specified time in the **Details** sub-tab of each of the threads.

More information about the dialog of ProfileDocumentEditor is as follows:

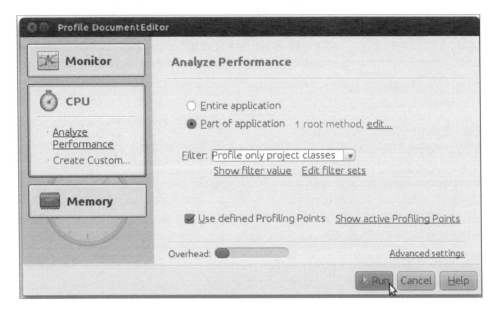

When the **Run** button is clicked another window is shown, containing all the controls for the profiling session.

From here it is possible to:

- ▶ Control garbage collection
- ▶ Save profiling snapshots
- ▶ Have a telemetry overview
- ▶ Check threads
- ▶ Start/stop profiling

The two options presented in the **Analyze Performance** section are:

- ▶ **Entire Application Data** generated by method invocation and exit is analyzed and presented. The bigger the application being profiled, the higher the overhead.
- ▶ **Part of Application analyzes** a more limited subset of the application, which is of course associated with lower overheads than when the entire application is profiled.

Both of the options will return real-time data.

To see some of the data produced by the CPU profiling session, navigate to the profiler window and search for the **Live Results** button. Click on it and **Live Profiling Results** will be shown:

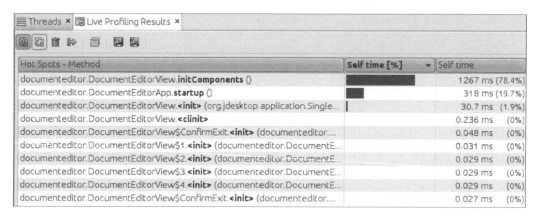

This data results from the time spent in each method, given in both percentage and milliseconds. The number of invocations is also shown in the profiler, which in our case turns out to be one, since we are only checking the startup method.

On **Analyzing Memory**, NetBeans maps all types, number of instances, and size of the created instances.

This mapping can be more or less specialized depending on which option was selected at the start of the profiling.

If a more specialized information set is required then **Record** both **Object creation** and **garbage collection**. For our example we are recording object creation only.

For the **Tracking every number of allocations** option we are using **1** which records all information. If using another number, say 5, each interval of 5 created objects will be recorded.

Using this option might degrade performance on slow machines since the amount of data produced is greatly increased, especially if huge production projects are being tested this way. Probably a better way would be to start off profiling subsets of the code instead of requiring all information at once.

After profiling the application it is possible to save snapshots for future references or for comparison.

It is possible to get a better visualization of the whole picture by comparing the application's performance in different circumstances and behavior.

More information is introduced in the *There's more* section of some of the topics covered in this recipe.

There's more...

Calibrating and detaching the NetBeans profiler.

Profiler calibration

Calibrating the profiler ensures that the current installed Java platform will provide more accurate results when dealing with bytecode compiled by the specific version of the JDK installed.

Please be aware that calibrating the profiler with laptops may lead to variable results due to dynamic frequency switching. Also avoid running calibration when the computer is under a heavy load, CPU/memory-wise; also, for more accurate results, run calibration only and close other programs.

Although it is necessary to calibrate the Profiler only once if only one version of the JDK is used, this requirement is no longer true if many different versions of JDK are installed. NetBeans will ensure that calibration occurs if none was ever made for that installed JDK.

VM telemetry overview

By placing the mouse cursor for a prolonged time over one of the graphs NetBeans will display more information related to that particular graph, as shown in the following screenshot:

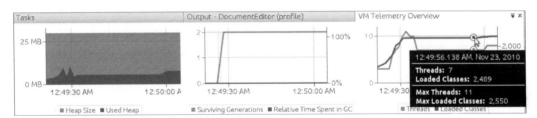

Comparing profiling snapshots

To compare profiling snapshots:

1. Launch the **Memory Profiler** one more time.
2. Click inside of the **Live Profiling Results** and select the icon **Take a Snapshot**.
3. Inside of the **Memory** locator press *Ctrl+S* to save.
4. Then navigate to **Profile...** located on the toolbar and select **Compare Memory Snapshots**. Snapshots are saved in the project folder. Snapshots are stored in `nbproject/private/profiler` in the project folder.

5. Select both snapshots.

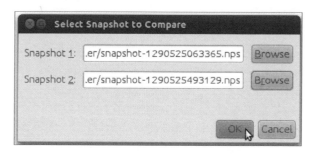

6. Click **OK**.

The IDE presents the result window, called **Liveness Comparision**:

Class Name - Live Allocated Ob...	Live B... ▲	Live Bytes	Live Obj...	Allocate...	Avg. Age	Generati...
char[]		-446,320...	-14,026	+101,143	+4.7	+1
java.lang.**Object**[]		-179,992...	-7,595	+59,573	+2.9	+2
java.lang.reflect.**Method**		-167,360...	-2,092	0	+1.4	-3
java.lang.**String**		-167,328...	-6,972	+50,472	+4.8	+1
java.util.**HashMap$Entry**		-83,736 B	-3,489	+26,456	+4.8	+2

Comparison of 05:11:03 PM to 05:18:13 PM

This presents the developer with differences in live objects, bytes, and averages; useful for finding memory hogs throughout the application.

By comparing memory snapshots, developers are able to identify how the application behaves in different kinds of testing and under different loads.

Creating unit tests

NetBeans can easily automate the task of creating skeleton **unit tests** for our classes.

In this process the IDE can write an entire unit class based on the available methods of some code. This class can be given different configurations with just a single click.

NetBeans integrates by default two different versions of JUnit by default. It is up to the developer to choose the most familiar one.

The biggest difference between versions is that JUnit 4 relies heavily on features introduced by Java 5, such as generics and annotations. Be aware that to use JUnit 4 the minimum JDK requirement is version 5.

Getting ready

For this recipe we will need a Java class with testable methods.

To start with JUnit we will need a Java project:

1. Create a new project, this can be achieved by either clicking **File** and then **New Project** or pressing *Ctrl+Shift+N*.

2. On **New Project** window on categories side choose **Java** and on Projects side select **Java Application** and click **Next >**.

3. Under **Name and Location**: Name the project as **JUnitApp**.

4. De-select the **Create Main Class** option.

5. Click **Finish**.

After project creation we will add a Java class that will be tested.

1. Right-click the default package of our JUnitApp.

2. Select **New** and **Java Class...**.

3. Name it as **Person** and click **Finish**.

We will then proceed to add fields in `Person.java`. To do this, replace the content of it with the following code:

```java
public class Person {
    String name;
    int age;
}
```

Then let's encapsulate the fields and create a `greet()` method:

1. Right-click the body of `Person.java` then select **Refactor...** and **Encapsulate Fields...**.

2. Click on **Select All** button and then the **Refactor** button.

Once the code has been refactored as the last method of the class, enter the following:

```java
public String greet() {
    return "Hi, my name is " + name + "and I am " + age + ".\nNice
to meet you!";
}
```

Save the class.

How to do it...

Now let's start creating JUnit tests:

1. Right-click on the **Project** under **JUnitApp** project and select **New** and **Other...**.

2. On **New Project** window on categories side choose **JUnit** and on File Type select **Test for Existing Class** and click **Next >**.

3. Under **Existing Class to Test**, click on the **Browse...** button, and on the **Select Class** dialog expand the default package, select **Person.java** and click **OK**.

4. Leave all the default options marked and click **Finish**.

New Test for Existing Class should look like the following screenshot:

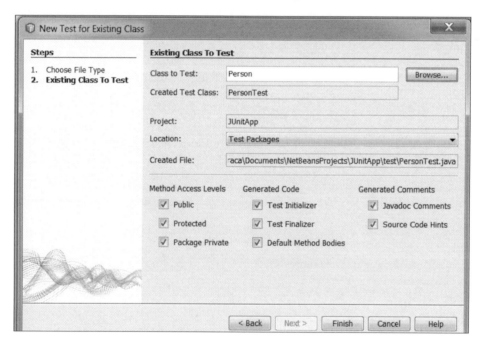

1. Select **JUnit 4.x** and click **Select**.

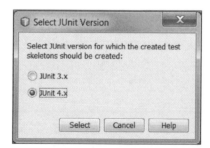

Now remove the results of the default behavior. In all of the methods remove the following:

```
// TODO review the generated test code and remove the default call to
fail.
fail("The test case is a prototype.");
```

In `testGetName()` replace:

```
String expResult = "";
```

with:

```
String expResult = "John";
instance.setName(expResult);
```

In `testSetName()` replace:

```
String name = "";
```

with:

```
String name = "John";
```

In `testGetAge()` replace:

```
int expResult = 0;
```

with:

```
int expResult = 30;
instance.setAge(expResult);
```

In `testGreet()`, replace the whole body of the method with the following:

```
System.out.println("greet");
Person instance = new Person();
String name = "John";
instance.setName(name);
int age = 30;
instance.setAge(age);
String expResult = "Hi, my name is " + name + "and I am " + age + ".\
nNice to meet you!";
String result = instance.greet();
assertEquals(expResult, result);
```

Save `PersonTest.java` and press *Shift+F6* to run the class.

How it works...

NetBeans creates the PersonTest under the **Test Packages** view of **Projects** window.

The IDE also adds the under Test Libraries the JUnit jar library.

If executing the tests once they were created will fail since they were all marked with the following:

```
// TODO review the generated test code and remove the default call to
fail.
fail("The test case is a prototype.");
```

But since we have removed the above line and inserted our code, we will see something like this when tests finish their execution:

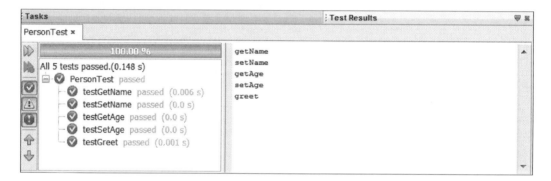

On the previous screenshot we can see on the left-hand side the name of the executed methods and their status, all marked with green for success, and on the right-hand side the output created by the `System.out.println()` calls within the named methods.

There's more...

When the project grows in size and the unit classes spread like wildfire it becomes more and more cumbersome to navigate through the endless maze of packages, and can take some time to find the respective class (or test class for that matter) which corresponds to the one we are working with.

NetBeans developers have therefore come up with a useful shortcut that improves the handling of those classes.

Suppose `Person.java` is open and we wish to open its JUnit-generated test class. Simply press *Ctrl+Shift+T* and the NetBeans will open `PersonTest.java` for you. Alternatively it is also possible to navigate back to the other class, say you wish to quickly modify something during the test phase, pressing the shortcut again will bring you back to `Person.java`.

Using SQE for improved code quality

Definition from the Software Quality Environment (SQE) home page:

"SQE attempts to provide first-class NetBeans IDE integration for different software quality tools".

```
http://kenai.com/projects/sqe/pages/Home
```

The different tools contained in the package are:

- ▶ FindBugs
- ▶ PMD
- ▶ CheckStyle
- ▶ Dependency Finder

This enables the developers to have code defect analysis, metrics, and dependency analysis.

Please be aware that this is an unstable module. Use at your own risk.

Getting ready

In order to use SQE we will first need to install the plugins.

1. Navigate to **Tools** and then **Plugins**.
2. On the **Plugins** dialog click on the **Settings** tab.
3. There, on the right side you will find an **Add** button, click on it.
4. Fill the **Update Center Customizer Name** with **SQE** and **URL** with
   ```
   http://deadlock.netbeans.org/hudson/job/sqe/lastStableBuild/
   artifact/build/full-sqe-updatecenter/updates.xml
   ``` then click **OK**.

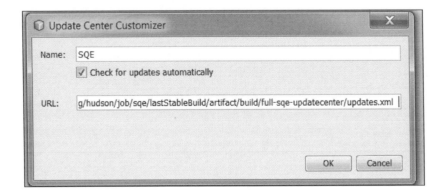

Note that SQE is added to the list of Configuration of Update Centers.

1. Now click on the **Available Plugins** tab and click on the **Reload Catalog** button.

2. Organize the **Packages by Category** and look for **Quality** on the category column.

3. Right-click in one of the four packages under Category name, (**PMD**, **FindBugs**, **Checkstyle**, **Depedency Finder**) and select **Check Category Quality**.

4. And click the **Install** button.

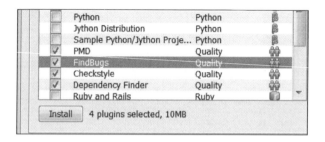

5. Follow the installation steps by accepting the **License Agreement** and on **Validation Warning**, click **continue**.

6. On the dialog where NetBeans informs the user that the plugins were successfully installed click **Finish**.

7. Then close the **Plugin Manager**.

The Toolbar is updated with both icons and another entry named Quality, as seen in the following screenshot:

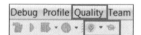

SQE can be used with your current project or any valid NetBeans project, but for this recipe we will use one of the projects that come bundled with NetBeans itself.

1. Create a New Project, by either clicking **File** and then **New Project** or pressing *Ctrl+Shift+N*.

2. On **New Project** window on categories side choose **Samples** and Java **Web** and on Projects side select **Servlet Examples (J2EE 1.4)** and click **Next >**.

3. Under **Name and Location**: Leave all the default values and click **Finish**.

## How to do it...

Select the **ServletExamples** project and on the toolbar click on **Quality** then **Code Defects** and finally **Run All Quality Tools**.

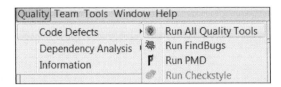

Let SQE perform the code checks.

## How it works...

SQE controls and views are displayed under the Java editor in the main view of NetBeans.

In our example **PMD** and **FindBugs** are shown with separate windows each.

Inside of each of those views, **PMD** or **FindBugs**, there are controls for how the visualization of the collected data is presented.

Controls such as:

- ▶ Bug instances by class/package
- ▶ Expand/Collapse All nodes in the tree

The PMD view presents a list of rule sets, for example `AppendCharacterWithChar` that were triggered in the project when code checks were performed. Opening one of these rule sets will present the developer with a list of classes, organized by packages, and the location of the code that is not in accordance with the rules.

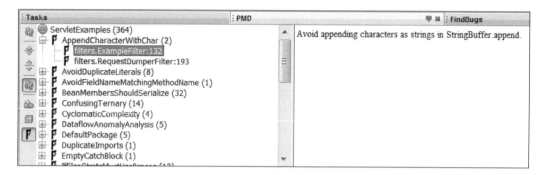

Double-clicking one of these results will take the developer to the class itself, specifically to the line where the problem is.

The right-hand pane of the PMD view also gives advice on how to eliminate this inconsistency.

**FindBugs** is the same:

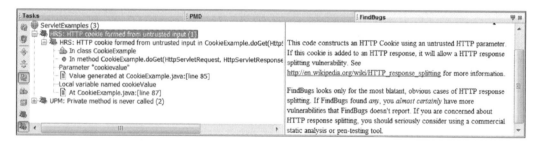

Possible bugs that were introduced in the code are listed. On the left-hand side the location and code snippet, and on the right-hand side the explanation of the problem.

The organization of FindBugs is a little different from PMD view but the principle of showing a guiding text on the right-hand side of the pane, and where to find the defect, is unaltered.

## There's more...

The quality control center displays a nice graphical snapshot of current problems with the project. Multiple projects can also be selected on this view. To access it, please click on **Window**, then **Quality**, and **QCC**.

It is a nice way to compare previous iterations of the project, to see how many issues are left and how many were corrected.

Complete with a **code defect dashboard** where a bar graph shows the issues by method and a code defect timeline.

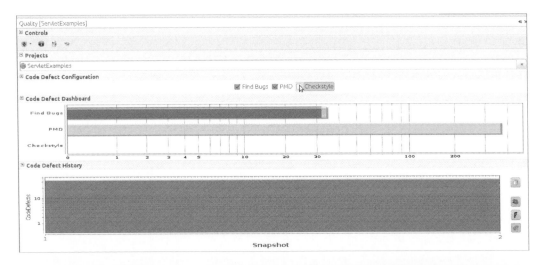

# Monitoring HTTP connections

Another tool that NetBeans provides users without all of the fuss of installing many different plugins and configuration files is the **HTTP Server Monitor**.

Although basic it mostly covers the main needs of a developer on the day-to-day case.

The NetBeans HTTP Server Monitor helps the developer to interact with HTTP requests, analyze cookies and headers, save and replay sessions, and more.

## Getting ready

NetBeans HTTP Monitor is enabled by default if the project is deployed onto Apache Tomcat.

This is a bit different if using GlassFish.

Since we will use GlassFish for this recipe follow the instructions below:

1. Navigate to the **Services** window.
2. Expand the **Servers** node, right-click on **GlassFish Server** and select **Properties**.

3. On **Servers** dialog under the **Common** tab select **Enable HTTP Monitor**.

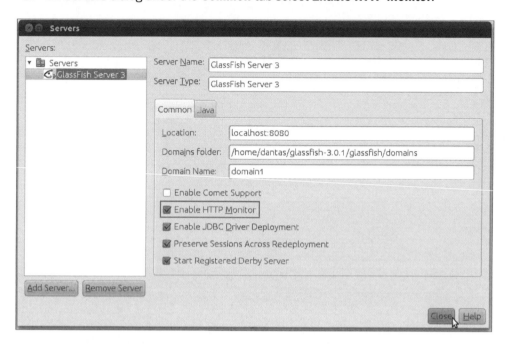

4. Click **Close**.

## How to do it...

Now follow the steps below to create a project that will be used to demonstrate the HTTP Monitor:

1. Create a New Project, by either; clicking **File** and then **New Project** or pressing *Ctrl+Shift+N*.

2. On **New Project** window on categories side choose **Java Web** and on Projects side select **Web Application** and click **Next >**.

3. Under **Name and Location**: Name the project as WebApplicationCookbook and click **Next >**.

4. Under **Server and Settings**: Click **Finish**.

5. With the project created, right-click **WebApplicationCookbook** and select **Run**.

## How it works...

When running the application, NetBeans fires up the **HTTP Server Monitor** (if it's not visible, hit *Ctrl+Shift+5*). The **HTTP Server Monitor** is used to analyze the information that is exchanged between the browser and the Application Server in real-time.

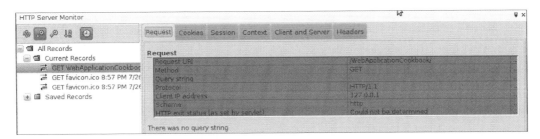

On the left-hand side of the panel, under **Current Records**, are listed the requests made from the client to the browser. By clicking on a request, the information related to that particular request is presented. There are a number of tabs that can be used to filter the information:

► Request

► Cookies

► Session

► Context

► Client and Server

► Headers

## There's more...

It is possible to edit requests and re-use them.

### Editing HTTP requests from within NetBeans

It is also possible to right-click on each individual request and choose **Save**, **Replay**, **Edit and Replay...**, and **Delete**.

To perform any of these actions, right-click on the request and choose the desired action.

The **Save** action will move the request from the **Current Records** folder into the **Saved Records**:

Replay will re-send the selected request to the server. This is useful when checking the outcome of the selected functionality.

Selecting **Edit and Replay...**, will let the user edit the request, change parameters, request methods, request URI, and so on before re-sending.

The **Edit and Replay** tab lets the developer add query parameters simply by clicking the **Add Parameter** button, then selecting a name and value for the given parameter.

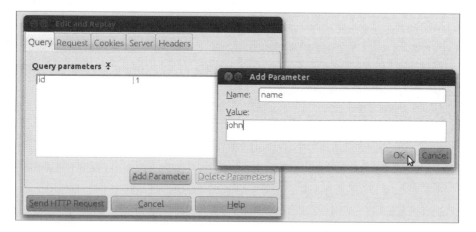

The **Request** tab gives the developer the power to change the request to one of these three HTTP request methods:

▶ PUT

▶ POST

▶ GET

Changing the **URI** and the **Protocol** can be done by double-clicking the rightmost part of the parameter in the UI.

This will make the IDE pop up a dialog asking for the corrected value.

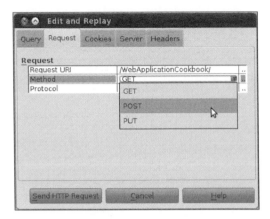

The **Cookies** tab, as with the **Query** tab, has a very straightforward operation; click on the **Add Cookie** button and enter the request information to add a cookie to your next request.

The **Server** tab relates to where the request will be heading. Mostly this information won't change since the development and deployment is done mainly on the localhost machine, but supposing that some machine in the same network might also be holding the application this is where to "redirect" the request to the other machine.

Here Hostname and Port Number of HTTP Service are the options. Double-clicking the rightmost part of the row, denoted by the three dots (...), will display a dialog where the information can be changed.

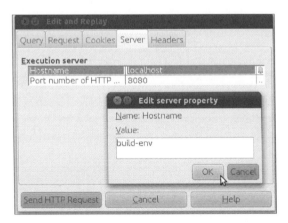

Various headers are present in the **Headers** tab and the addition, editing, and deletion of headers is possible.

Both addition and deletion can be executed by the down most buttons and the edition by double-click the rightmost part of the row, denoted by the three dots (...).

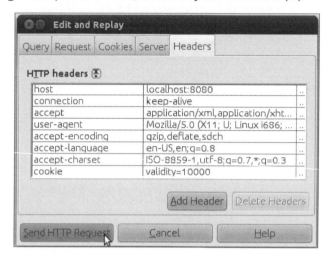

Once a request has been edited, just click on **Send HTTP Request** and the modified request will be on its way.

# Using the JMeter load generator

JMeter is another cross-platform tool under the Apache umbrella.

It is typically used as a load testing tool for web applications, although with the integration of different plugins it is possible to extend it to better suit your needs.

JMeter uses a .jmx extension as the testing plan and we will see how to use NetBeans plugins to create and load those files from within the IDE.

In this recipe we will see how to create and run JMX plans from within the IDE. The creation and configuration of such plans are beyond the scope of this book.

If you wish to know more about Apache JMeter please visit: http://jakarta.apache.org/jmeter/.

## Getting ready

We will need two plugins for controlling JMeter from within NetBeans.

These plugins are:

- ▶ JMeter Kit
- ▶ Load Generator

Both can be found from the **Plugin Manager**:

To do so, follow the below steps:

1.  Navigate to **Tools** and then **Plugins**.
2.  On the **Plugin Manager** dialog click on **Available Plugins**.
3.  Click on **search** and type **load generator**.

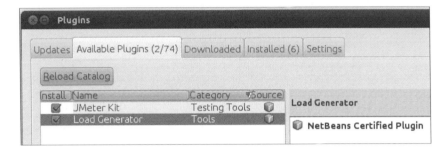

4.  Select both plugins and click on the **Install** button.
5.  Accept the license agreement and follow the installation process.
6.  Close the **Plugin Manager**.

We will need a Java Web project for this recipe to continue. Follow the steps below for creating one:

1.  Create a New Project, this can be achieved by either clicking **File** and then **New Project** or pressing *Ctrl+Shift+N*.
2.  On **New Project** window on categories side choose **Samples** and **Java Web** and on Projects side select **Servlet Stateless (Java EE 6)** and click **Next >**.
3.  Under **Name and Location**: Leave all the default values and click **Finish**.

## How to do it...

Now we will create a JMeter Plan:

1.  Right-click on **Servlet Stateless** node, select **New** and **Other....**

2. On **New File** dialog under **Categories** expand the **Load Testing Scripts** node and click on the **JMeter Plans** folder.

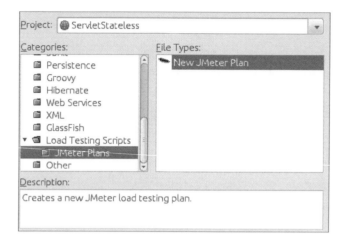

3. Then on **File Types** select **New JMeter Plan** and click **Next**.

4. Under **Name and Location**: under **Script Name** type **TestingPlan** and let the IDE take care of the other fields.

5. Click **Finish**.

With our JMeter plan created, let's load a test script.

1. Click on the **Services** window.

2. Expand the **Load Generator** node, right-click on it and press **Start...**.

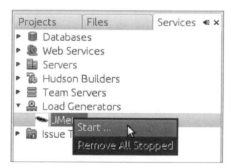

3. You will be prompted with a **File Chooser**.

4. Navigate to the **jmeter** folder in the **StatelessServlet** project and select the **.jmx** file.

5. Click **OK**.

## How it works...

When loading the JMX file NetBeans will execute it and display the following text on the output window:

*Starting JMeter subsystem... Done*

*Starting JMeter test plan named JMeter Template Plan (/home/user/ NetBeans Cookbook/Chap 11/ServletStateless/jmeter/TestingPlan.jmx)*

*Simulating 2 users with ramp-up time of 3s*

*JMeter test plan running*

*JMeter test plan stopped*

## There's more...

Editing JMX files and another way of using a load generator in NetBeans.

### JMeter+NetBeans profiler

It is also possible to start JMeter by using NetBeans Profiler.

To do this follow the steps below:

1.  On the toolbar click on **Profile...** and then **Profile Main Project** (or press *Alt+F2*).
2.  Select the Java SDK used for profiling and press **OK**.
3.  On **Profile ServletStateless** dialog you will notice a checkbox for the **LoadGenerator Script**, check it.

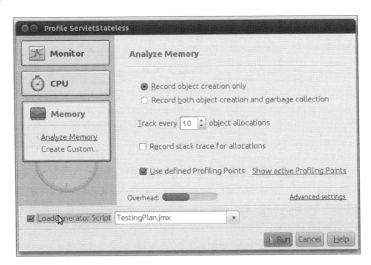

4. The profiler shows the scripts associated with this project.

5. To execute the script in conjunction with the profiler click **Run**.

## Editing the JMX file

Right-clicking on the .jmx and selecting **External Editing** will bring up the JMeter editor.

This is where you will be able to create the Load Generator Script properly.

# 12
# Version Control

In this chapter, we will cover:

- ▶ Adding a project to Subversion
- ▶ Checking in modifications
- ▶ Working with a Subversion branch
- ▶ Resolving conflicts in Subversion
- ▶ Creating a Mercurial project
- ▶ Cloning a Mercurial repository
- ▶ Committing to a Mercurial project

## Introduction

Version control systems are widely used in industry since they provide the development team with a central point where code can be uploaded (committed), and checked for differences, changes can be rolled back, other development branches created, the list can go on and on.

In this chapter we will see how to use two of the most popular Version Control Systems on the market with NetBeans, using the IDE instead of external applications to do the work.

## Adding a project to Subversion

Apache Subversion is a free, cross-platform version control system developed by the Apache Foundation, intended as successor to CVS (which is still available in NetBeans).

If you wish to know more about Subversion please visit:

`http://subversion.apache.org/`

Here we will see how to add a connection to a Subversion server.

## Getting ready

In this recipe we will assume that no Subversion server is available on the local machine.

So for this recipe to work we will need to visit and create an account at `http://sourceforge.net`.

Sourceforge offers free SVN repositories; it has limited capabilities but will be perfect for our needs.

To create a project, follow the steps below:

1.  Create a New Project, this can be achieved by either clicking **File** and then **New Project** or by pressing *Ctrl+Shift+N*.

2.  On **New Project** window on categories side choose **Java** and on Projects side select **Java Application** and click **Next >**.

3.  Under **Name and Location**: Under **Project Name** enter **NBCookbookSVN** and click **Finish**.

Once the account and a new project have been created in Sourceforge we need to configure NetBeans to use Subversion. To do this, follow the steps below.

Note that the steps below might not be necessary if SVN is already installed in the system path:

1.  On the toolbar click on **Tools** then **Options**.

2.  In the **Options** dialog click on the **Miscellaneous** button.

3.  Then click on the **Versioning** tab.

4.  Under **Versioning Systems** click on **Subversion**.

5.  Navigate to Subversion's installation folder by clicking **Browse...** and select it.

6. Back on the **Options** dialog click **OK**.

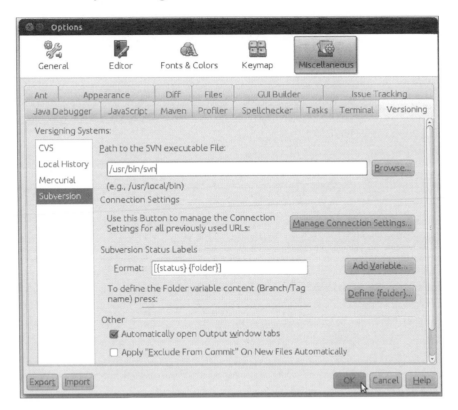

All the steps provided in this recipe can also be performed with your own Subversion server of choice such as (open-source) Google Code or e.g. your company's internal SVN server, for example.

## How to do it...

To start we will need to add the project to Subversion. Here are the steps to do it:

1. Right-click **NBCookbookSVN** node, select **Versioning** and **Import into Subversion Repository...**.

2. Under **Subversion Repository**: Enter the repository **URL** (the one provided by Sourceforge when account was created), **user** and **Password**.

3. Click **Next**.

4. Under **Repository Folder**: Leave the **Repository Folder** with its default value and under **Specify the Message** field enter **Project Creation** and click **Next**.

5. And finally on **Files to import** leave all the files selected and click on **Finish**.

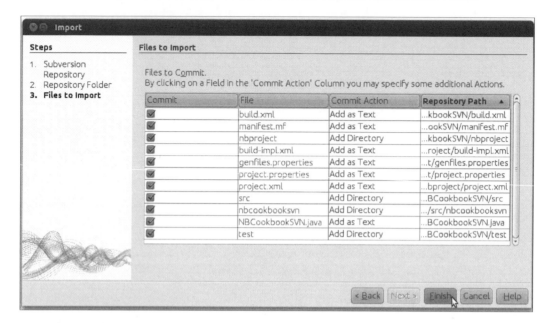

## How it works...

NetBeans acts as a mediator between Subversion and the user, abstracting all of the manual commands in favor of a simplified UI.

So when NetBeans needs to send all of the locally-created code to Sourceforge's server, all the work is hidden from the user, although on the status bar it is possible to see a progress bar indicating that the IDE is sending the code.

# Checking in modifications

After creating and adding a project with Subversion the next step is to send the code and file modifications to it.

## Getting ready

For this recipe we will need a Subversion server or an account from some Subversion provider, such as Sourceforge.

Configuring NetBeans accordingly to work with Subversion and a Java project are necessary for this recipe.

For explanations on how to create a Subversion account on Sourceforge and add a project to Subversion, refer to the *Getting Ready* section in the beginning of this chapter.

This recipe can also be used with a previously created project, in the case of on-going development.

## How to do it...

Carry out the following steps in order to delete NBCookbookSVN.java:

1. Right-click on the .java file and select **Delete**.
2. On the **Delete** dialog check **Safe Delete** and click on **Refactor**.

In order to add a new class you will have to execute the following steps:

1. Right-click on the **Sources Package**, select **New** and **Java Class...**.
2. On the **New Java Class** dialog, under **Name and Location** enter **Class Name** as **Person**.
3. Enter nbcookbooksvn as **Package** and click on **Finish**.

And finally, to commit the changes:

1. Right-click on the **Sources Package**, then **Subversion** and **Commit...**.
2. On the **Commit** dialog, under **Commit Message**, enter **First commit** and click on the **Commit** button.

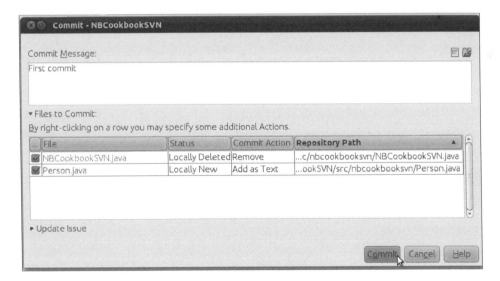

## How it works...

Adding and deleting a file are two distinct actions that are usually performed by Subversion in the command line.

So when we commit all changes we are not just sending the files to the server, but also deleting and creating new ones on it.

It works the same way whether only code is added, files modified or files deleted/created.

NetBeans highlights files with different colors depending on whether they are new, marked for deletion, or have modifications.

The colors are:

- ▶ **Gray**: Shows that the current file is not yet sent to version control.
- ▶ **Blue**: When the local file was modified.
- ▶ **Green**: Shows that the file has been added locally.
- ▶ **Red**: Conflicts between the local and server copy of the file.

The same coloring scheme can be related to lines of code inside a file. Code lines can also be marked with blue, green, and red indicating the same behavior as explained in the bullet points above.

In the following screenshot NetBeans shows the archives that are synced with the server and not-modified with the blue icon.

Note that `Person.java` is written in with a green color, since it is a newly added locally, and `NBCookbookSVN.java` is marked as gray.

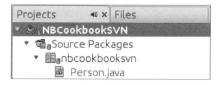

The little blue icon looking like a small glass means that changes (creation, modification, and deletion) have occurred to the indicated package.

Since `Person.java` was not sent to the server, the file is shown without the blue icon.

## There's more...

Ways to track changes in the code the and NetBeans **diff** window are explained as follows.

### Show changes

Many times, changes to one particular feature in the project affect many different files. So many that it is hard to keep track of what has been changed.

To see the changes to the local files compared to the ones in the server is easy:

1. Right-click on the **Source Packages** node.
2. Select **Subversion** and **Show Changes**.
3. A new view is launched.

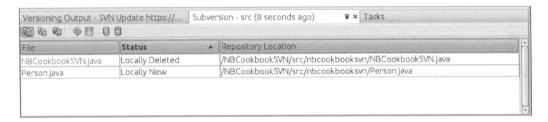

We can see which files were altered, the status of these files, and the path.

The icons placed on top of the Subversion view are there to help the developer filter the view of the changes.

The first three actions, represented by the icons (left to right) are:

- ▶ Show Both Locally and Remotely Modified Files
- ▶ Show Locally Modified Files
- ▶ Show Remotely Modified Files

These three icons will change the way the files are presented in the view.

The other four icons are:

They are responsible for the following actions (left to right):

- ▶ **Refresh Status**: Checks if there was any other modifications to files
- ▶ **Diff All**: Opens a window, same place where the code editor is, with the changes for the listed files
- ▶ **Update All**: Brings the latest changes from the server to the local copy
- ▶ **Commit All**: Sends all the local changes to the server

So besides the previously mentioned way of committing changes to Subversion, this window provides another way of doing it.

## Diff window

The Diff window is where all the differences between the local copy and the copy on the svn server are shown.

It is possible to call this window by clicking on the **Diff All** button when **Show Changes** pane is on, or by right-clicking the project node then selecting **Subversion** and finally **Diff**.

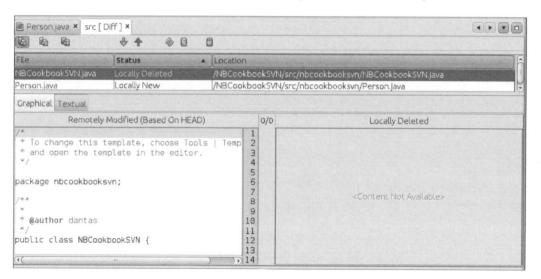

The screenshot above shows those modifications and the path of each one of those. The left and right panes show the specific locations where modifications were made in both local and remote files.

# Working with a Subversion branch

In case you are not familiar, a Subversion **branch** is a different line of development which has the contents copied from the main line and is, therefore, identical to it until more development is done on this new branch.

The typical case is where the developer creates a branch to used for bugfixes to a version with no further development planned while the main branch, or HEAD, goes on with new features.

This recipe will show how to create a branch.

## Getting ready

For more information on how to setup NetBeans and Subversion, please, refer to the first *Getting Ready* section at the beginning of this chapter.

## How to do it...

Let's perform the following steps to create a new branch:

1. Right-click on the project node and select **Subversion** and **Copy To...**.
2. On **Repository Location** click on **Browse...**.
3. Once **Browse for Repository** Folders pops-up and loads, select the root node and click **Into a new Folder**.
4. On the **Specify New Folder** enter NBCookbookSVN-V1 and click **OK**.
5. Back on browse **Repository Folders**, click **OK**.

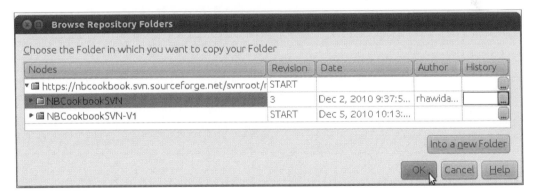

6. Then on the **Copy** window enter a **Copy Description**, such as Release 01-01-2011 and click **Copy**.

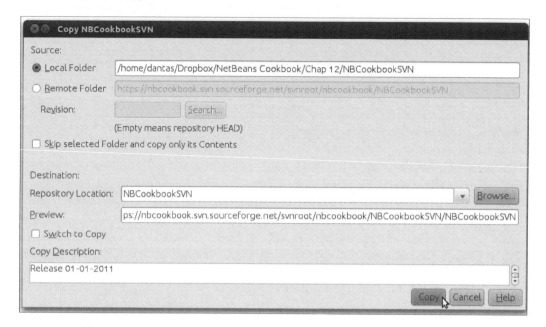

## How it works...

By visiting your Subversion server, in our case Sourceforge, we can check that the branch was successfully created.

## There's more...

Merging a branch back into MAIN.

### Merging branches

Branching a project is very important for all the benefits that it brings, such as fixing certain bugs or introducing features specific for some usage. And more often than not we will need to fold those changes back into the main development line. The action of integrating those changes is called **merging**.

Merging can become quite tricky when product development is far down the line. Especially if that merging is done through the command-line. Having the IDE do some of the hard work and presenting the user with detailed notifications could come in handy.

On this matter NetBeans also includes support for the merging technique.

To perform the merge:

1. Right-click the project node, select **Subversion** and **Merge Changes...**.

2. When the **Merge Changes** window opens, under **Merge From** select **One Repository Folder**.

3. Then under **Repository Folder** click on **Browse...**.

4. On **Browse Repository Folders** select the desired branch, which in our case is the one we have created, and click **OK**.

5. Back on **Merge Changes** window leave the other fields with their default values and click **Merge**.

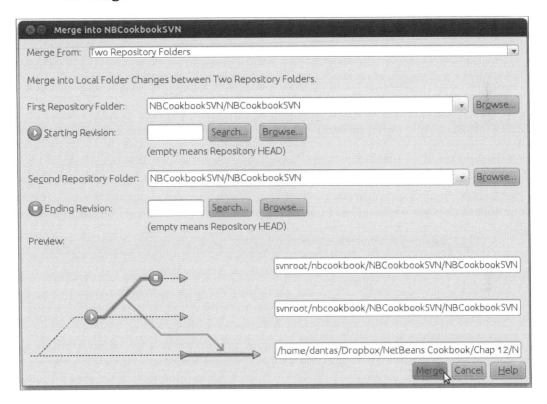

The action we have just performed will bring changes from one of the repository.

Other options provided by NetBeans include bringing changes from **Two Repository Folders**, as shown in the following screenshot:

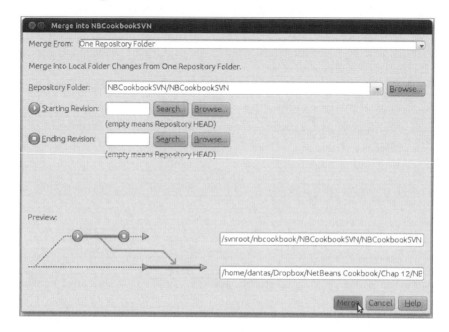

And the **One Repository Folder Since its Origin** option brings changes from the user-specified revision number and when the branch was created:

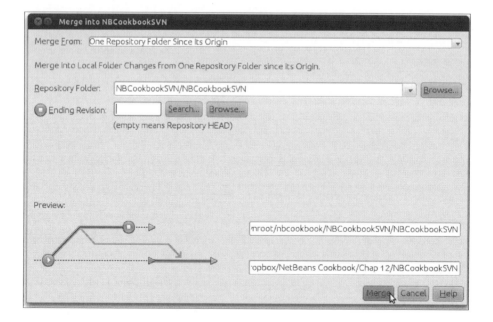

# Resolving conflicts in Subversion

Code conflicts will arise when the local copy has different contents in the same location as the content that is present in the server.

The resolution of conflicts in version control systems is a painful fact that every developer must face sooner or later.

Let's check how to solve code conflicts with Subversion and NetBeans.

## Getting ready

For more information on how to setup NetBeans and Subversion, please refer to the first *Getting Ready* section at the beginning of this chapter.

How to do it...

1.  Right-click the project node, select **Subversion** and **Resolve Conflicts...**.
2.  The **Merge Conflicts Resolvers** pops-up, click on the code to be accepted and then on **OK**.
3.  Choose the correct option by clicking on **Accept** and click on **OK**.

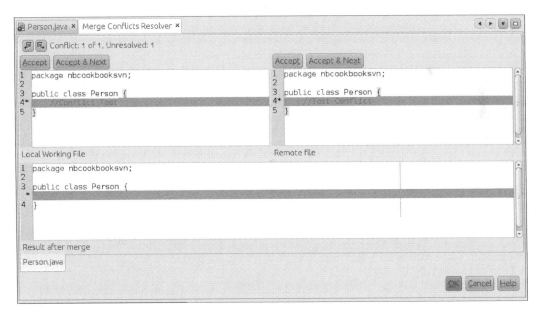

4.  When asked to **Save**, click on **Yes**.

## How it works...

As mentioned in the introduction of this recipe, a conflict will arise whenever different code is present in the same line in both local and remote copies. In the previous screenshot we have introduced conflicts.

NetBeans presents the developer with a window divided in three parts. The Local Working File is the file which we are editing and, most probably, started the conflict; the Remote File is the one in the Subversion server; and the Result After Merge, the lower pane, is how the file will look after the conflict is resolved.

In our particular case we resolve the conflict by accepting the changes from the server and merging them, automatically, when the **Accept** button on the Remote File side was clicked.

In the following screenshot, blue indicates changes since the first version, and green that changes that have been added since the previous version. Red indicates lines removed since the previous version.

Resolving conflicts turns the previously red highlighted sections of code into blue and green.

# Creating a Mercurial project

Mercurial is one of the new breed of version control systems called **DVCS (Distributed Version Control Systems)** that use distributed repositories residing in every developers machine, instead of centralized ones as is the case with Subversion.

Let's take a look at how to integrate Mercurial and NetBeans.

## Getting ready

In this recipe we will assume that no Mercurial repository is available on the local machine.

We first need to create an account in a Mercurial repository provider.

So for this recipe to work we will need to visit and create an account in `http://sourceforge.net`.

Under Sourceforge we will host our free Mercurial repositories, which will be enough for our needs.

Keep in mind that, while using Sourceforge to test this recipe, it is necessary to enable Mercurial since it is not enabled by default.

Visit the link below for more information:

`https://sourceforge.net/apps/trac/sourceforge/wiki/`
`Mercurial#Management`

Once the account and a new project have been created in Sourceforge, we need to configure NetBeans to use Mercurial.

1. On the toolbar click on **Tools** then **Options**.
2. In the **Options** dialog click on the **Miscellaneous** button.
3. Then click on the **Versioning** tab.
4. Under **Versioning Systems** click on **Mercurial**.
5. Navigate to Mercurials's installation folder by clicking **Browse...** and select it.
6. Leave all the other options with their default values and click **OK**.

We will now have to configure the Mercurial repository in NetBeans.

On the toolbar click on **Team**, then **Mercurial** and **Properties**.

Enter the Mercurial **default-pull**, **default-push**, and **username** to the dialog box and click on **OK**.

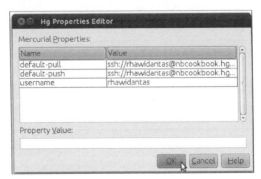

Carry out the following steps in order to create a project:

1. Create a New Project, by either clicking on **File** and then **New Project** by pressing *Ctrl+Shift+N*.

2. On **New Project** window on categories side choose **Java** and on Projects side select **Java Application** and click **Next >**.

3. Under **Name and Location**: Under Project Name enter **NBCookbookHG** and click **Finish**.

## How to do it...

Now to initialize our project:

1. Right-click project node, select **Mercurial** and **Initialize Mercurial Project**.

2. On the **Repository root path** click leave the default value and click **OK**.

3. In order to commit your project: Right-click on the project and select **Mercurial** then select **Commit...**.

4. On the commit window under **Commit Message** enter **first commit**, then click on **commit**.

## How it works...

Once the repository has been configured NetBeans will perform a check against the Mercurial server. When this is finished, the project in NetBeans will look slightly different.

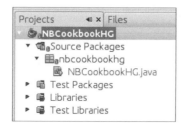

The file highlighted in green denotes that it is a new file that has not yet been committed to the server.

The little blue icon looking like a small glass means that changes (creation, modification, and deletion) have occurred to the indicated package.

## There's more...

Let's check the server for modifications.

### Status of server files

Before doing the commit it is possible to have a look at the status of the newly-created project.

This is useful to check changes against the server and find out which files have been created, deleted, or modified.

1. Right-click on the project node.

2. Select **Mercurial** then **Status**.

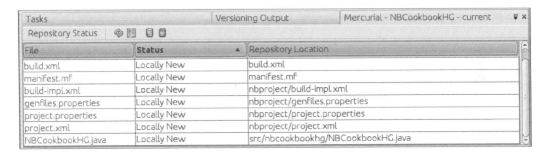

# Cloning a Mercurial repository

Cloning a repository means that the developer will take the version of the files from a certain point in time, the time of the cloning, and will make a copy of those files. This new cloned repository is a totally complete and independent local copy of the one contained in the server.

Note that cloning is not the same thing as branching in other version control systems. This feature is very useful when experimentations are needed with the code but the risk of wrecking an already working copy of the files in the local machine comes up. This way we can make as many mistakes without the risk of ruining our own work space.

## Getting ready

For more information on how to get the Mercurial sources and repositories up and running for this recipe, please, refer to the *Getting Ready* section of the *Creating a Mercurial Project* recipe in this chapter.

## How to do it...

On the toolbar click on **Team**, **Mercurial**, and **Clone <Project Name>** (in our case **NBCookbookHG**.

On the **Clone Repository** window change the **Parent Directory** to some different folder and click on **Clone**.

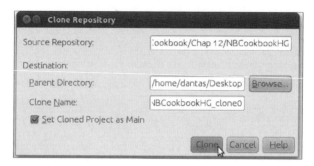

## How it works...

NetBeans will then copy the contents from the **NBCookbookHG** into the newly created folder **NBCookbookHG_clone0**.

This name can be modified in the Clone Repository window to reflect the reason of the repository cloning. Let's say, a version 1 of the product.

# Committing to a Mercurial project

After changing the files and making sure that everything is working properly the developer will want to send those changes to the server.

In this recipe we will see how to do this using Mercurial.

## Getting ready

For more information on how to get the Mercurial sources and repositories up and running for this recipe, please refer to the *Getting Ready* section of the *Creating a Mercurial Project* recipe in this chapter.

## How to do it...

To delete a file follow the steps below:

1. Expand the **Project** node, **Source Packages**, and **nbcookbookhg**.

2. Right-click on the `NBCookbookHG.java` and select **Delete**.

3. On the **Delete Window** choose **Safe Delete** option and click on **Refactor**.

To create a file:

1. Right-click on the now empty **nbcookbookhg** package and select **New** and **Java Class...**.

2. On the **New Java Class** window under **Name and Location**, write under Class Name Car and click **Finish**.

3. Enter the following code inside of `Car.java`.

```
String model;
String plate;
int year;
int price;
String color;
```

4. Save it.

To commit code:

1. Right-click on the project node and select **Mercurial** and **Commit...**.

2. On the **Commit** window enter as **Commit Message**, first commit and click on **Commit**.

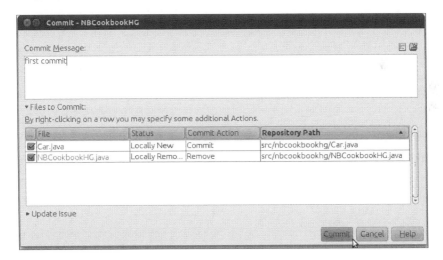

How it works...

By clicking on the **Commit** button NetBeans sends the modifications to the Mercurial server.

NetBeans interfaces with Mercurial on behalf of the user to abstract all the command line work with a simple and intuitive UI.

There's more...

Need to revert to a certain version?

For moments when that commit did not sit so well

To revert to an earlier version execute the following steps:

1. Right-click on the project node, select **Mercurial** and **Revert...**.

2. The **Revert Modifications** window presents the developer with the latest commit.

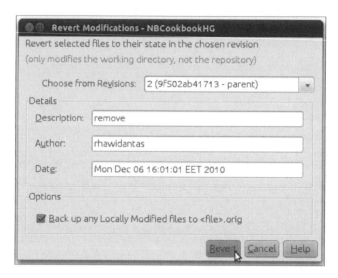

3. On the **Revert Modifications** window on the **Choose from Revisions** select the desired revision and click on **Revert**.

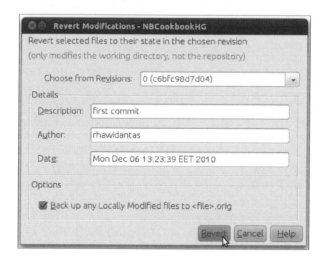

Index

Thank you for buying
NetBeans IDE 7 Cookbook

About Packt Publishing

Packt, pronounced 'packed', published its first book "*Mastering phpMyAdmin for Effective MySQL Management*" in April 2004 and subsequently continued to specialize in publishing highly focused books on specific technologies and solutions.

Our books and publications share the experiences of your fellow IT professionals in adapting and customizing today's systems, applications, and frameworks. Our solution based books give you the knowledge and power to customize the software and technologies you're using to get the job done. Packt books are more specific and less general than the IT books you have seen in the past. Our unique business model allows us to bring you more focused information, giving you more of what you need to know, and less of what you don't.

Packt is a modern, yet unique publishing company, which focuses on producing quality, cutting-edge books for communities of developers, administrators, and newbies alike. For more information, please visit our website: www.packtpub.com.

About Packt Open Source

In 2010, Packt launched two new brands, Packt Open Source and Packt Enterprise, in order to continue its focus on specialization. This book is part of the Packt Open Source brand, home to books published on software built around Open Source licences, and offering information to anybody from advanced developers to budding web designers. The Open Source brand also runs Packt's Open Source Royalty Scheme, by which Packt gives a royalty to each Open Source project about whose software a book is sold.

Writing for Packt

We welcome all inquiries from people who are interested in authoring. Book proposals should be sent to author@packtpub.com. If your book idea is still at an early stage and you would like to discuss it first before writing a formal book proposal, contact us; one of our commissioning editors will get in touch with you.

We're not just looking for published authors; if you have strong technical skills but no writing experience, our experienced editors can help you develop a writing career, or simply get some additional reward for your expertise.

Building SOA-Based Composite Applications Using
NetBeans IDE 6

Design, build, test, and debug service-oriented applications with ease using XML, BPEL, and Java web services

David Salter   Frank Jennings   PACKT

Building SOA-Based Composite Applications Using NetBeans IDE 6

ISBN: 978-1-847192-62-2   Paperback: 300 pages

Design, build, test, and debug service-oriented applications with ease using XML, BPEL, and Java web services

1. SOA concepts and BPEL process fundamentals

2. Build complex SOA applications

3. Design schemas and architect solutions

4. JBI components including service engines and binding components

5. Master the BPEL Designer, WSDL Editor, and XML Schema Designer

Java EE 5
Development With NetBeans 6

Develop professional enterprise Java EE 5 applications quickly and easily with this popular IDE

David R. Heffelfinger   PACKT

Java EE 5 Development with NetBeans 6

ISBN: 978-1-847195-46-3   Paperback: 400 pages

Develop professional enterprise Java EE applications quickly and easily with this popular IDE

1. Use features of the popular NetBeans IDE to improve Java EE development

2. Careful instructions and screenshots lead you through the options available

3. Covers the major Java EE APIs such as JSF, EJB 3 and JPA, and how to work with them in NetBeans

Please check **www.PacktPub.com** for information on our titles

NetBeans Platform 6.9 Developer's Guide

ISBN: 978-1-849511-76-6 Paperback: 288 pages

Create professional desktop rich-client Swing applications using the world's only modular Swing application framework

1. Create large, scalable, modular Swing applications from scratch

2. Master a broad range of topics essential to have in your desktop application development toolkit, right from conceptualization to distribution

3. Pursue an easy-to-follow sequential and tutorial approach that builds to a complete Swing application

Magento 1.4 Development Cookbook

ISBN: 978-1-84951-144-5 Paperback: 268 pages

Extend your Magento store to the optimum level by developing modules and widgets

1. Develop Modules and Extensions for Magento 1.4 using PHP with ease

2. Socialize your store by writing custom modules and widgets to drive in more customers

3. Achieve a tremendous performance boost by applying powerful techniques such as YSlow, PageSpeed, and Siege

4. Part of Packt's Cookbook series: Each recipe is a carefully organized sequence of instructions to complete the task as efficiently as possible

Please check **www.PacktPub.com** for information on our titles

iReport 3.7

ISBN: 978-1-847198-80-8   Paperback: 236 pages

Learn how to use iReport to create, design, format, and export reports

1. A step-by-step, example-oriented tutorial with lots of screenshots to guide the reader seamlessly through the book

2. Generate enterprise-level reports using iReport 3.7

3. Give your reports a professional look with built in templates

4. Create master/detail reports easily with the sub-report feature

RESTful Java Web Services

ISBN: 978-1-847196-46-0   Paperback: 256 pages

Master core REST concepts and create RESTful web services in Java

1. Build powerful and flexible RESTful web services in Java using the most popular Java RESTful frameworks to date (Restlet, JAX-RS based frameworks Jersey and RESTEasy, and Struts 2)

2. Master the concepts to help you design and implement RESTful web services

3. Plenty of screenshots and clear explanations to facilitate learning

4. A developer's guide with practical examples to ensure proper understanding of all concepts and the differences between the frameworks studied

Please check **www.PacktPub.com** for information on our titles

Java EE 6 with GlassFish 3 Application Server

ISBN: 978-1-849510-36-3   Paperback: 488 pages

A practical guide to install and configure the GlassFish 3 Application Server and develop Java EE 6 applications to be deployed to this server

1. Install and configure the GlassFish 3 Application Server and develop Java EE 6 applications to be deployed to this server

2. Specialize in all major Java EE 6 APIs, including new additions to the specification such as CDI and JAX-RS

3. Use GlassFish v3 application server and gain enterprise reliability and performance with less complexity

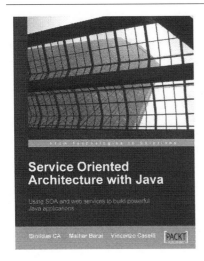

Service Oriented Architecture with Java

ISBN: 978-1-847193-21-6   Paperback: 192 pages

Using SOA and web services to build powerful Java applications

1. Build effective SOA applications with Java Web Services

2. Quick reference guide with best-practice design examples

3. Understand SOA concepts from core with examples

4. Design scalable inter-enterprise communication

Please check **www.PacktPub.com** for information on our titles

Printed in Great Britain
by Amazon.co.uk, Ltd.,
Marston Gate.